STUDENT IMPACT

MW00388779

WALKING

WITH

CHRIST

TWELVE
LESSONS
THAT WILL
CHANGE
YOUR LIFE

VOLUME ONE
Small Group
RESOURCES

BO BOSHERS
*Tricia Murphy, Troy Murphy
and Kristin Smith*

ZondervanPublishingHouse
Grand Rapids, Michigan
A Division of HarperCollins*Publishers*

WILLOW CREEK
RESOURCES

I would like to dedicate this curriculum to each of you with a shepherd's heart who has been called by God to serve high school students. I pray that the small groups on these pages will be a powerful resource for gathering students together and putting them on the path to becoming fully devoted followers of Christ. May God richly bless you for following the call He's placed on your heart to impact the lives of students ... you are making a difference.

Serving together, one life at a time,
Bo

Walking with Christ © 1997 by The Willow Creek Association

Requests for information should be addressed to:
ZondervanPublishingHouse
Grand Rapids, Michigan 49530

ISBN: 0–310–20124–1

Interior design by Jack Rogers

Printed in the United States of America

98 99 00 01 02 03 04 /❖ ML/ 10 9 8 7 6 5 4

CONTENTS

ACKNOWLEDGMENTS

I would like to recognize and express my thanks to those who were instrumental in making this project happen.

To Tricia Murphy, who used her creativity, devotion, and desire to capture God's Truth for the result of moving students practically to find the love of Christ. Thank you for your friendship and sensitivity.

To Troy Murphy, my lifelong friend, who used his artistic gifts to help create the right format for sharing this resource. Thank you for your devotion to this project; I love running the race with you.

To Bruce and Kristin Smith, for their service as part of the original team that visualized this project and helped bring it about. We have built some great memories of team and friendship.

To Erin Frazier, who joined the team through her willingness to take a step of adventure in using her gift of writing. Thank you for your contribution and promptness; I hope there are more projects for us to do together in the future.

To Lynette Rubin, my friend and assistant, for her availability, support, and willingness to adjust when I needed it. I could not have done this without you.

To Dave Lambert, Rachel Boers, Jane Vogel, and their teams at Zondervan, who gave us understanding, support, patience, and direction in developing this project. Thank you for your time and energy.

And to the Willow Creek Association team, for the many people who were involved in making this desire for small group curriculum a reality. Thank you for the privilege of doing this project with you. Together we have all seen a dream come true.

You are holding in your hands an exciting tool! It's not every day that you can find a tool that will:
- assist you in touching the lives of high school students with whom you are involved—as a full-time, part-time, or volunteer youth leader;
- equip you to talk to your students in ways that will allow them to experience God in more intimate ways; and
- change the way you develop small groups in your student ministry.

Walk through the next few pages and catch the vision for this tool that will help you make a difference in the lives of high school students.

The next few pages are devoted to sharing a vision for small groups in student ministry. You will discover how small groups can most effectively be used to bring about life changes and specifically how to implement small groups using the experiences in this book. Take plenty of time to reflect on the impact these opportunities for community and growth can have on the students whose lives you influence.

WHY SMALL GROUPS?

Change—The Purpose of Small Groups

Small groups are essential to the development of spiritual life in those who want to be fully devoted followers of Christ. They are essential because community, growth, sharing, and discipleship happen in the context of a group. In Student Impact, the high school ministry of Willow Creek Community Church in Barrington, Illinois, we refer to our small groups as D-Teams (with the "D" representing the Greek word *Delta*, meaning "change.") Our mission is simply to turn irreligious high school students into fully devoted followers of Christ.

To accomplish this mission, Student Impact is based on a seven-step strategy. Everything we do fits into this strategy:

1. Integrity Friendship

    The process begins as we challenge our core students to build "relational bridges" with their non-Christian friends.

2. Verbal Witness

    After students have built credible friendships with their non-Christian friends, we teach them to look for opportunities to explain and discuss their relationship with Christ.

3. Supplemental Witness: Providing a Service for Seekers

    Student Impact, our service for seekers, is designed to nurture students' spiritual interest by introducing them to the message of Christ in a contemporary and relevant way. Impact is intended to be used as a tool by our core in reaching their non-Christian friends by supplementing their ongoing witness.

4. Spiritual Challenge

    At this stage of their friendship, we teach our core students to ask pointed questions that intentionally challenge their friends to consider the claims of Christ. We believe that once a seeker has spent time listening to God's Word and observing fully devoted Christian students, he will discover through the conviction of the Holy Spirit his need for a personal relationship with Jesus Christ.

5. Integration into the Body

   Student Insight, our worship service for believers, is designed to mature the believer on the trek toward full devotion to Christ. Insight provides believers with an opportunity to participate in corporate worship and to listen to expository Bible teaching.

6. Discipleship Through Small Groups

   Small groups provide a discipleship atmosphere. From this small group comes accountability, encouragement, and support, as well as Biblical teaching through learning experiences.

7. Ownership

   At this stage of spiritual development, students are taking an active role in service within the church. Through both financial giving and using their spiritual gifts, they are owning their part of the Lord's work. A student now steps forward and takes the role of evangelist within his own circle of influence and thus begins a third spiritual generation. This occurs as he takes his non-Christian friends through the same seven steps he traveled.

The vision of Student Impact is to create a unique community of students and leaders committed to letting God

- change their lives;
- change their friends' lives;
- build the church; and
- impact the world.

The four volumes of small group experiences, *Walking with Christ*, *Compassion for Lost People*, *Learning to Serve*, and *A Lifelong Calling*, are written with these four values (we call them "waves" of ministry) in mind. This book of experiences focuses on the first wave of life change: a personal relationship with Jesus Christ. A student must experience Gods' grace and accept Christ's payment for sin to begin on the road to becoming a fully devoted follower. We strongly believe that students want to understand what Christ did through both His life and death. This volume will assist you in communicating that truth.

For fuller development of how small groups fit into the vision and mission of student ministry, see *Student Ministry for the 21st Century: Transforming Your Youth Group into a Vital Student Ministry* by Bo Boshers with Kim Anderson (Zondervan, 1997).

Authenticity—Leading by Example

As the leader of small group life, your role is not only to teach the Word of God but to be an example to your students. It's more than talking. It's living in the moment with students, thinking the way they think, asking questions that allow them to reflect on their world, creating an environment that provides opportunities for uninterrupted community and soul-searching. These moments are about helping students take the time to look at Christ and grow to be more like Him. It's about life change.

In Student Impact, D-Teams meet every other week. But our walk with Christ is lived out daily. Today's students are looking for leaders who live authentic lives in Christ. As a leader, you not only facilitate the D-Team experiences, but you work to help students view the world from God's perspective each day. The greatest lesson students learn is not from these materials but from your life. This can happen only through your commitment of time, prayer, and preparation. The D-Team experiences in this book will serve as the basis for group interaction, but the key to fully devoted followership is allowing God to work through you so that students experience Him.

If you're unfamiliar with the D-Team format, take a few minutes to read the following overview.

HOW TO USE THIS BOOK

For each small group meeting, you'll find Leader's Notes that will guide you through your preparation and actual leading of the group experience, and Student Notes that you can photocopy and distribute to your students to use during your time together. The Student Notes are designed so that you can photocopy the two pages back-to-back, then fold them to form a four-page booklet that your students can slip easily into their Bibles. (You'll notice that the page numbers in the Student Notes look out of order when they are unassembled.) Encourage your students to take their notes home, perhaps filing them in a notebook or binder, so they can look back at what they've learned throughout their small group experiences.

The Leader's Notes contain all the information in the Student Notes plus the following features to help you prepare and lead your students.

Unit Introduction

Each unit begins with an introduction that includes the Leader Focus and Big Picture. The Leader Focus will help you begin thinking about the unit theme from a new perspective. In the Big Picture, you'll find a brief description of the values and objectives for each unit as well as the D-Team experiences themselves. You'll also get your first look at the Unit Memory Verse. Each unit builds on the one before, but you can also use the units independently if that's more appropriate for your time frame or the needs of your particular students. You'll notice that the lessons within each unit are numbered independent of the other units to give you this flexibility.

Before the D-Team Experience

Each session has an easy-to-use summary outline that will help you see the D-Team experience at a glance.
*   *Leader Devotion*—To impact students at the deepest level, there can be no mistaking the value of a leader's personal authenticity. The heart of the leader is key. This section will challenge you to recall personal experiences and gain new insights that you can share with your students. This mini-devotion will prepare you for the role of leadership.
*   *Student Focus*—This section provides the leader with the rationale for the D-Team experience. It provides clarification on what a student can expect if he or she is committed to this experience and the truths to be learned. It may also provide an opening discussion question.
*   *Unit Memory Verse*—Only four memory verses appear in each volume. When students focus on memorizing one verse per unit, they will truly have ownership of that verse and can apply it to their lives on a daily basis.
*   *Practical Impact*—We believe students learn best when they experience God's truth, not just talk about it. Each Practical Impact section outlines ways for students not only to hear the Word of God, but to experience it.
*   *Materials Needed*—Here you will find a list of everything you need to bring to the D-Team experience. Student Notes are provided for each D-Team experience and can be duplicated back-to-back for your D-Team members. Encourage your students to keep these notes in a binder so they can look back on what they've learned.
*   *Special Preparation*—In this section, you will find detailed instructions to help you prepare for your D-Team experience. Phone contacts, letters, reproducible handouts, suggestions about advance phone contacts and letters, and other ideas for resources will help ensure that your D-Team experience goes smoothly.
*   *Environment*—Because students are sometimes more able to freely experience God outside the context of four walls, each D-Team experience offers two options. Option 1 works in any setting, while Option 2 moves the experience outside a normal meeting room to an environment that has been created specially for the D-Team. Option 2 takes time and thought on the part of the leader, but it can set up a D-Team experience in a very powerful way. Explore your options. Figure out what freedom you have in this area. Depending on the size or structure of your student ministry, the environment can be established in different ways. If a large number of students meet together before they divide into different D-Teams, a master teacher approach can help to establish the environment by "painting a picture," then dismissing students.

Leading the D-Team Experience (60 min.)

Your entire D-Team experience should last approximately 60 minutes. It's divided into four sections: Get Started (5 minutes), The Experience (40 minutes), Reflection (5 minutes), and Make an Impact (10 minutes). Questions and Scriptures that are **bold-face and italic** in your Leader's Notes are duplicated in the Student Notes.

Get Started (5 min.)

During the first five minutes of the first D-Team experience of each unit, you will help your students: preview the objectives of the unit; understand the Unit Memory Verse; spend some time in prayer; and discover what to expect in this D-Team experience. In the next two D-Team experiences of each unit, you will use this time to review assignments and challenges from the previous D-Team experiences, encourage student-led prayer, and share objectives for the new D-Team experience.

The Experience (40 min.)

This forty-minute section is broken down into several steps to help you lead the experience. This is the practical work and discussion section for the students. You'll find step-by-step instructions along with discussion questions, Bible study, activities, and various practical exercises. Feel free to insert your own thoughts and insights—things God showed you during your Leader Devotion time as well as in your general preparation for the D-Team experience.

Reflection (5 min.)

This five-minute portion of the experience will help your group members solidify the truths they have learned as they reflect individually on the experience. Encourage your D-Team members to truly invest in this section. Model for them the value of reflection as you work through the questions listed here. Don't be afraid of the silence of reflection as opportunities for growth are being formed in students' minds! Model openness in your own personal application, but especially encourage your D-Team members to share their ideas on how to apply the truths in their lives. Use the Summary Statements to reinforce the truths the students have learned.

Make an Impact (10 min.)

During the last ten minutes of your D-Team experience, you have the opportunity to challenge your students to make personal applications of the principles they have experienced. Don't forget to seek God's guidance for each of your students.

• *... In Your Life*—Students like to be challenged. This section allows you to offer some sort of assignment and challenge to your D-Team members. Let them know they have a choice in accepting the challenges. Make it inviting to commit, but not easy. Remind your students that it takes training to develop godly character (1 Tim. 4:7b-8) that will bear fruit.

• *... With Accountability*—In this section, you will encourage each student to choose another person in the D-Team as an accountability partner. Together, they will work on the Unit Memory Verse. In addition, accountability partners will have opportunities to share their responses to assignments and challenges.

• *Prayer*—Be sure to close the D-Team experience in prayer. Model the value of prayer by upholding it before and after each D-Team experience. Invite your students to pray as they are comfortable. Explore this opportunity to pray in community with your D-Team members if you find that they are hesitant to pray aloud. You may ask certain students to pray for specific areas as you sense the development of community and safety.

FOLLOW UP

If you have more than one small group, you can use the Shepherding Summary Form (page 111) to enable communication between D-Team leaders and the ministry director. Duplicate this form and have each D-Team Leader in your student ministry fill it out after each D-Team experience. Simply indicate brief responses to the questions in each section. Over time, this process will assist you in accountability, opportunities for encouragement, record-keeping for D-Team member information, and direction-setting for your student ministry leader.

Unit 1 Introduction

LEADER FOCUS

If a stranger approached you and asked, "What can you tell me about who Jesus is?" how would you respond? Would your answer draw the person to a place where he or she would want to know more about this Jesus who you know on an intimate level? Jesus asked His disciples: "Who do people say I am?" (Mark 8:27) Before you continue in your preparation for the D-Team experiences in this unit, take a few minutes and reflect on the answer you would give that stranger. May your understanding of who Jesus is be stretched in new and exciting ways as you lead your students to walk as Jesus walked.

BIG PICTURE

Unit Overview
In Unit 1 we will be focusing on learning how to walk with Jesus by answering three questions: (1) Who is Jesus? (2) Why follow Jesus? (3) How do I follow Jesus?

1. "Who Do You Say I Am?"
During this D-Team experience, your students will discover the opportunity to know Jesus by making three life-changing decisions:

    Decision #1: To meet Jesus
    Decision #2: To get to know Jesus
    Decision #3: To respond to Jesus

2. Reason to Follow
During this D-Team experience, your students will discover two compelling reasons for following Jesus:

    Reason #1: We all have a spiritual thirst.
    Reason #2: Jesus is the Source that can fill our thirst.

3. The Two-Step
During this D-Team experience, your students will discover how they can follow Jesus by taking two steps of obedience:

    Step #1: Go to Jesus.
    Step #2: *Then* make adjustments.

STUDENT
IMPACT

Unit Memory Verse
"Whoever claims to live in him must walk as Jesus did" (1 John 2:6)

Unit 1 Introduction

"Who Do You Say I Am?"

Before the D-Team Experience

LEADER DEVOTION

Read Luke 5:4–8. Picture it. Peter had worked all night long without catching a single fish. His muscles were sore, and he was tired and sweaty. Suddenly, Jesus suggested something that seemed ridiculous—"Let down the nets." Peter chose to obey and was overwhelmed by the results. Fish everywhere! So many fish that the nets broke and the boats began to sink! In response, all Peter could do was drop to his knees and acknowledge Jesus as Lord.

Think back to *your* first encounter with Jesus. How did Jesus grab your attention? What kinds of feelings did you experience in your first encounter with Him? Were you humbled by Jesus' presence as Peter was? In what areas of your life did you experience an increased sense of awareness about yourself?

Prepare your own heart for leading this first D-Team experience by writing a letter or starting a journal to express your thanks to Jesus for revealing Himself to you. Then spend some time reflecting on His Lordship in your life by focusing on the Unit Memory Verse: 1 John 2:6. As you prepare for this D-Team experience, jot down your personal experiences and insights in the "Prep Notes" column so you can share them with the students. You might want to record your responses to the following questions: Are there areas of my life that I need to put back in Jesus' hands? What are they? Am I holding on to a relationship, a job, or any sin patterns that I need to surrender to Jesus?

Before you encourage your students to make Jesus Lord, make sure you have surrendered control of your own life, and are following the Leader.

LOOKING AHEAD

Student Focus
Every D-Team member will discover the way to know Jesus by making three life-changing decisions:

Decision #1: To meet Jesus
Decision #2: To get to know Jesus
Decision #3: To respond to Jesus

Unit Memory Verse
"Whoever claims to live in him must walk as Jesus did" (1 John 2:6).

Practical Impact
At the end of this D-Team experience, your students will make a cross, using the materials with which you have supplied them. As they read the story of Christ's death on their own this week, this powerful time of reflection will encourage them to decide if Christ is truly Lord in their lives.

BE PREPARED

Materials Needed
- Bibles and pens
- Duplicated Student Notes
- Your own personal objects for the opening discussion
- Modeling clay, masonry nails, wire, wood, string, felt-tip pens, etc., for making crosses

Special Preparation
- Contact your D-Team members in advance and remind them to bring their Bibles (if they have them). Ask them to bring one or two personal belongings that reveal something about who they are. Suggest the following items: a high school yearbook, awards, trophies, artwork, music, sports equipment, family pictures, etc.
- Read Matthew 16:13–16 and be prepared to share the story of Peter's confession in your own words.

Environment
To set up the environment for this D-Team experience, you can choose one of the following. Option 1 works in any setting; Option 2 moves the experience outside your normal setting.

Option 1: This D-Team experience opens with the question, "Who are you?" Use the personal objects suggested under "Special Preparation" to know one another as well as to set up your study about Jesus.

Option 2: Since you will be studying the story of Peter's first encounter with Jesus, you may want to have your D-Team meet outdoors near a lake, pond, or maybe even in a boat! Bring the personal objects with you.

Leading the D-Team Experience
(60 min. total)

| GET STARTED |

Unit Preview
Have a student read aloud the information under the "Preview" in the Student Notes:
As you work together through "Unit 1: Follow the Leader," you will discover how to walk with Jesus by answering three life-changing questions:
1. *Who is Jesus?*
2. *Why follow Jesus?*
3. *How do I follow Jesus?*

Unit Memory Verse
Read aloud 1 John 2:6, "Whoever claims to live in him must walk as Jesus did," and explain that the proof of a believer's fellowship with God is found in a life modeled after that of Jesus.

Student Prayer
Ask a student to pray that each D-Team member will have open ears and an open heart to what Jesus wants him or her to know about Himself.

Focus
Share with your D-Team members that this week every member will discover the way to know Jesus by making three life-changing decisions:

Decision #1: To meet Jesus
Decision #2: To get to know Jesus
Decision #3: To respond to Jesus

| THE EXPERIENCE |

Decision #1: To meet Jesus
Introduce Decision #1 by asking the question: "Who are you?" Display the personal items that you brought. Share how these objects reveal something about who you are. Be open and transparent as you describe yourself. Then ask each student to display his or her personal item and answer the question: "Who are you?"

After each person has had a chance to answer the question, explain that together you will be exploring the answer to this same question about Jesus.

Briefly paraphrase Peter's confession of Christ as found in Matthew 16:13–16. Explain that when Jesus asked Peter, "Who do you say I am?" Peter replied, "You are the Christ, the Son of the living God." The story of Peter's confession of Christ leads us to several questions: How did Peter know who Jesus was? And more important, How do we know who Jesus is? Each of us can know who Jesus is by making the first of the life-changing decisions mentioned previously—to meet Jesus.

Have your D-Team members *read Luke 5:1–11.* Ask a student to read the verses aloud. Then discuss the following questions:

What words would you use to describe Peter before he met Jesus? (fisherman, hard worker, boat owner, frustrated, hospitable)

What words do you think Peter would have used to describe Jesus prior to the big catch? (teacher, ordinary man, confident, a good speaker, commanding)

How would you describe Peter after he met Jesus? (humbled, astonished, generous, obedient, aware of his sinfulness and unworthiness, follower, fearful)

In what ways did Peter's perspective on Jesus change? (When Jesus met Peter's specific need for a big catch, Peter's eyes were opened to Jesus' power; Peter knew and acknowledged Jesus as Lord.)

What happened the first time you met Jesus? Ask several volunteers to share their experiences.

Decision #2: To get to know Jesus
Explain that Peter's life was never the same after he met Jesus. He answered Jesus' call, left his job and family, and followed Him. Each day, Peter had the opportunity to see Jesus in action and see that Jesus was truly Lord. After we make the decision to meet Jesus, we have another decision in front of us: the decision to get to know Jesus. As we get to know Him, we will discover the answer to the question, "Who is Jesus?"

Assign each D-Team member one of the following verses. Ask each student to read the verse silently and then be prepared to share what Peter learned about Jesus as he got to know Him.

Matthew 4:23–25—Jesus is Teacher, Preacher, and Healer
Matthew 7:28–29—Jesus is a Teacher with authority
Matthew 8:14–17—Jesus is a caring, compassionate Healer; He has authority and power over demons, spirits, and sickness
Matthew 9:1–8—Jesus is able to forgive sins, know our thoughts, and heal paralysis
Matthew 9:10–13—Jesus is friendly, caring, and willing to share Himself with sinners and rejected outcasts
Matthew 10:1—Jesus specifically chooses His followers and gives them His authority over evil spirits and sickness
Matthew 16:16—Jesus is Christ, the Son of God

Explain that we are given the opportunity to get to know Jesus through prayer, obedience, and study of His Word. This often results in our learning something new about Him.

Ask your D-Team members to **write down one word that describes something they have recently learned or experienced about Jesus.** If time permits, allow each student to share what he or she has written.

Decision #3: To respond to Jesus
Emphasize that Peter walked, talked, ate with, and traveled with Jesus daily. He saw Jesus perform miracles, heard Jesus' teachings, and experienced change in his life through these events. Peter knew through personal experience that Jesus was more than just a good man, prophet, or great teacher. As a result, Peter made a third life-changing decision—to respond to Jesus.

Say: *Picture Peter falling to Jesus' knees and acknowledging Him as Lord. Are you daily responding to Jesus in the same way? In your heart, are you doing what Jesus is asking of you?*

Explain that when we respond to Jesus by making Him Lord of our lives, our lives are changed. As a result, we know the answer to the question, "Who do you say I am?" in a powerful and personal way.

Distribute materials and instruct D-Team members to take the next few minutes to make a cross. Ask them to reflect on the cross they make and answer the question, "Who is Jesus?" Suggest that they place their homemade crosses in a place where it will catch their attention during the week—next to their bed, inside their locker, or on a car dashboard. Every time they see the cross, they should ask themselves, "Who is Lord?"

REFLECTION

(5 min.)

Discuss the following questions:

If your friends or family had to say who you are, what word would they use to describe you?

Would they describe you simply by how you look or what you do? Or would they be able to see that Jesus is your Lord and that you are a follower of Him?

Is Jesus truly Lord over your friendships? Your dating relationships? Your family relationships? Your future? Your school plans and activities? Or are you trying to take control, solve problems, and make decisions on your own?

Give your students a few moments to record honest responses to the following questions, found in their Student Notes: *What was most meaningful to you about our experience today? What does God want you to do in response?*

Ask a student to read aloud the Summary Statements in the Student Notes.

Summary Statements

We learned today that . . .
- Jesus is Lord.
- We can get to know Jesus through prayer, obedience, and studying His Word.
- When we respond to Jesus, our lives are changed.

MAKE AN IMPACT

(10 min.)

. . . In Your Life
Challenge your D-Team members to set aside some quiet time this week to read Matthew 27:11–54. Encourage your students to reread the story and consider what Jesus has done for them. Emphasize that Jesus, the Son of God, humbled Himself to be a man and died on the cross so that He could be Lord in our lives.

Then encourage them to spend time this week in prayer or write a letter to Jesus thanking Him for revealing Himself. Ask group members to be ready to share what they have learned from this experience the next time you get together as a D-Team.

. . . With Accountability

Have the D-Team members form pairs to become accountability partners for the week and to work on the memory verse. Have each student begin learning the **Unit Memory Verse** by writing it out in the space provided in the Student Notes.

Prayer

Bring the students back together and close in prayer.

1. "Who Do You Say I Am?"

Preview
As you work together through "Unit 1: Follow the Leader," you will discover you can walk with Jesus by answering three life-changing questions:

1. Who is Jesus?
2. Why follow Jesus?
3. How do I follow Jesus?

Unit Memory Verse
"Whoever claims to live in him must walk as Jesus did" (1 John 2:6).

Focus
You will discover how to walk with Jesus by making three life-changing decisions.

THE EXPERIENCE

Decision #1: To meet Jesus
Read Luke 5:1–11. What words would you use to describe Peter before he met Jesus?

What words do you think Peter would have used to describe Jesus prior to the big catch?

How would you describe Peter after he met Jesus?

---

consider what Jesus has done for you. Do you realize that Jesus, the Son of God, humbled Himself to be a man and died on the cross so that He could be Lord in your life?

This week, reflect on the cross you have made and answer the question, "Who is Jesus?" Spend some time in prayer or write a letter to Jesus thanking Him for revealing Himself to you. Every time you see the cross, ask yourself, *Who is Lord?* Be ready to share what you have learned from this experience.

. . . With Accountability
With your accountability partner, talk about your responses to the "Reflection" questions. Exchange phone numbers. Call each other this week to hold each other accountable to making an impact in your life.

name _____

phone _____

Begin learning your memory verse by writing it out in the space below.

MEMORY VERSE
1 John 2:6

In what ways did Peter's perspective on Jesus change?

What happened the first time you met Jesus?

Decision #2: To get to know Jesus

Quietly read the verse you have been assigned and then be prepared to share what Peter learned about Jesus as he daily walked with Him.

Matthew 4:23–25—

Matthew 7:28–29—

Matthew 8:14–17—

Matthew 9:1–8—

Matthew 9:10–13—

Matthew 10:1—

Matthew 16:16—

Write down one word that describes something you have recently learned or experienced about Jesus.

Decision #3: To Respond to Jesus

Picture Peter falling to Jesus' knees and acknowledging Him as Lord. Are you daily responding to Jesus in the same way? In your heart, are you doing what Jesus is asking of you?

REFLECTION

If your friends or family had to say who you are, what word would they use to describe you? Would they describe you simply by how you look or what you do? Or would they be able to see that Jesus is your Lord and that you are a follower of Him?

Is Jesus truly Lord over your friendships? Your dating relationships? Your family relationships? Your future? Your school plans and activities? Or are you trying to take control, solve problems, and make decisions on your own?

What was most meaningful to you about our experience today?

What does God want you to do in response?

Summary Statements

We learned today that . . .
- Jesus is Lord.
- We can get to know Jesus through prayer, obedience, and studying His Word.
- When we respond to Jesus, our lives are changed.

MAKE AN IMPACT

. . . In Your Life

Set aside some quiet time this week to read Matthew 27:11–54 and

Reason to Follow

Before the D-Team Experience

LEADER DEVOTION

Webster's Dictionary defines the word *follow* in several ways: "to go or come after; to go in pursuit of; to act in accordance with; to succeed in order of time; to go or come after a person in place, time, or sequence, etc."

In our world, "to follow" does not sound very appealing. We want to lead and be in control. We want first place, not second or third. People in our world don't beat down the door to possess qualities like humbleness, obedience, self-sacrifice, and service. And yet, "follow Me" is Jesus' way. "Follow Me" is His plan. "Follow Me" is a command Jesus gives to His disciples then and now.

Webster's defines the word *follower* in these ways: "one in the service of another; an adherent, a disciple; a machine part that receives motion from another part; etc."

Jesus defined the word *follower* in the Gospel of Matthew: "Come to me, all you who are weary and burdened, and I will give you rest. Take my yoke upon you and learn from me, for I am gentle and humble in heart, and you will find rest for your souls. For my yoke is easy and my burden is light" (Matt. 11:28–30).

Why follow Jesus? When we choose to follow Jesus, He frees us from sin and burdens. Our "machines" now run on His power, not on our own. *Follow* actually means freedom and a future for you and me. As you prepare for this D-Team experience, think about the week you just finished. Did you experience the freedom, power, and rest that is available to you? Are you relying on Christ to fill your needs? Jot down your personal experiences and insights in the "Prep Notes" column so you can share them with the students.

During this D-Team experience, you will give students cups and ask them to reflect on whether or not they are filled by the love and power of Christ that is available when we follow Him. Imagine there is a cup of water in front of you now. How full is your cup?

LOOKING AHEAD

Student Focus
Every D-Team member will discover two compelling reasons for following Jesus:

Reason #1: We all have a spiritual thirst.
Reason #2: Jesus is the Source that can meet our thirst.

Unit Memory Verse
"Whoever claims to live in him must walk as Jesus did" (1 John 2:6).

Practical Impact
During this D-Team meeting, your students will experience physical thirst and then relate it to the spiritual thirst we all have known. By the end of your time together, your students will know that Jesus is the only Source who can fill their thirst, and they will be challenged to reflect on how Jesus quenches their thirst each day.

BE PREPARED

Materials Needed
- Bibles and pens
- Duplicated Student Notes
- Plastic cup for each D-Team member
- Pitcher of ice-cold water
- Optional: salty foods (chips, pretzels, popcorn)

Environment
To set up the environment for this D-Team experience, you can choose one of the following. Option 1 works in any setting; Option 2 moves the experience outside your normal setting.

Option 1: Meet in your normal setting and provide salty foods to create a thirst in your students.

Option 2: Since this D-Team meeting focuses on the Living Water that Jesus offers when we follow Him, meet in a place where people are thirsty, like a beach, track field, or basketball court. If time allows, take your students on a short run or lead them in aerobics.

Leading the D-Team Experience

(60 min. total)

GET STARTED

(5 min.) 🕐

Review
Last week you challenged your students to read the story of the crucifixion and reflect on the cross they made to help them remember who Jesus is and what He did for them. Discuss the following questions: *As you reflected on the cross you made, what did you learn about Jesus? Did you find yourself doing anything differently during the week as a result? In what ways were you encouraged or challenged?*

Student Prayer
Ask each pair of students to pray that the D-Team meeting will be a time of growth.

Focus
Share with your D-Team members that during this meeting every member will discover two compelling reasons for following Jesus:

Reason #1: We all have a spiritual thirst.
Reason #2: Jesus is the Source that can fill our thirst.

THE EXPERIENCE

(40 min.) 🕐

Reason #1: We all have a spiritual thirst.
Begin this D-Team experience by creating thirst in your students. You might offer them salty foods without anything to drink. Or you might have them imagine how fresh ice water would feel, taste, or look if they were stranded on a desert island.

After you have created thirst in your students, place a cup in front of each person. Fill the cups with ice-cold water and ask your students not to drink from the glasses. Then ask: "How does the water look? How would you feel if you could drink some right now? What would it taste like?" After your D-Team members respond, suggest these additional answers:
- The water looks refreshing!
- It looks as if it would quench my thirst.
- I'd give anything to have a sip.
- I need a drink to survive.
- I'll die if I don't get a drink.
- I don't want just a sip; I want to gulp the whole thing down.

Then explain how water is a necessity in our lives. People can live days without food, but not without water. History shows that the survival of villages, towns, and even nations depends on water. Share with your students that you're sure they're aware that everyone has a thirst for water, but note that everyone also has a spiritual thirst—for Living Water.

Have your students **read aloud John 4:1–42**—the story of a woman with a need for water. After reading the story, share with your students three obstacles that might have prevented Jesus from even talking with this woman.

Obstacle #1: *The woman was a Samaritan.*

Have your students look at verse 9. Point out that Jesus was traveling from Judea to Galilee. The shortest route between these two places was to walk through Samaria. The Samaritan race resulted from the interracial marriage of Jews and Assyrians. As a result, Jews viewed the Samaritans to be impure and did everything possible to avoid traveling through Samaria. But Jesus purposely chose to travel through Samaria.

Obstacle #2: *The woman was a known sinner.*

Have your students look at verses 16–18. Note that the Samaritan woman had five husbands and was living with a man who was not her husband. Refer to verse 6 and ask them what time of day the woman had come to the well. Point out that the woman came to the well at about the sixth hour or, in other words, at noon. Explain that people usually came to the well during the morning and evening. The Samaritan woman probably chose to come at this time because of her reputation.

Obstacle #3: *The woman was in a public place.*

Explain that at this time, a respectable man would have never talked to a woman with the reputation of the Samaritan woman.

Discuss the following question: **How would you describe the Samaritan woman's thirst (or needs)?** (She was searching, lonely, lacked respect, searching for love through relationships [five husbands], lacked hope for a bright future.)

Reason #2: Jesus is the Source that can fill our thirst.

Explain that the Samaritan woman came to the well to get water, but it became clear she needed much more. Like this woman, we all have thirst—we all have felt things like loneliness, insignificance, insecurity, fear, worry, hopelessness. There is only one Source that can completely quench our spiritual thirst. That Source is Jesus Christ.

Ask your students to think about the ways Jesus related to the woman. Then discuss the following questions: **What can you learn about Jesus from His encounter with the Samaritan woman?** (Jesus is not racist or sexist; all people matter to Jesus; He pursues people in spite of sin or reputation; He desires to have a relationship with us; He loves unconditionally.) **What did Jesus offer to this woman?** (More than drinking water; Living Water that forever quenches thirst; a spring of water welling up to eternal life; spiritual nourishment; a personal relationship with the Son of God.)

Emphasize that Jesus was the only Source who could fill this woman's needs. Ask: **Has there ever been a time when Jesus offered you something that filled your thirst or need?** To get your D-Team members started, share your own story.

Ask a volunteer to read John 4:39–42 aloud. Then summarize by noting that the result of Jesus' conversation with the Samaritan woman was that many of the Samaritans believed in Him and knew He was really the Savior of the world. Point out that when we look at all that Jesus offers us, the answer to the question, "Why follow Jesus?" becomes crystal clear: Reason #1 is that we all have a spiritual thirst, and Reason #2 is that Jesus is the only Source that can quench that thirst.

 (5 min.)

REFLECTION

Hold up one of the plastic cups. Ask your students to think about all that Jesus offers them. Remind them that Jesus desires to fill their cups to overflowing. **What are some of the ways Jesus has chosen to fill our spiritual thirst?** After giving your D-Team members an opportunity to respond, share some of the following ways:
- Jesus Christ, the Son of God, humbled Himself to be a man and died on the cross so He could meet our need for a Savior and Lord.

- He desires a personal relationship with us in spite of our sin.
- He loves us unconditionally.
- He knows us intimately, just as he knew the Samaritan woman who testified, "He told me everything I ever did."
- He strengthens and nourishes us.
- He offers freedom from our sin and eternal life.

Ask your students to write down something they thirst for in their lives.

Give your students a few moments to record honest responses to the following questions, found in their Student Notes: **What was most meaningful to you about our experience today? What does God want you to do in response?**

Ask a student to read aloud the Summary Statements in the Student Notes.

Summary Statements

We learned today that . . .
- Everyone has a spiritual thirst.
- Jesus is the Source that can meet our thirst.

MAKE AN IMPACT

(10 min.)

. . . In Your Life
As you hold up a plastic cup, encourage your D-Team members to let their cups be a reminder during the next week of why they follow Jesus. Encourage them to give their day to Jesus every morning and commit to following Him and letting Him fill their needs. Suggest that every evening, before they go to sleep, they write a word on the cup that represents how Jesus filled one of their needs during the day. It might be through an answered prayer, a special conversation, or experiencing Jesus' love and care through someone.

. . . With Accountability
Have the D-Team members form pairs to become accountability partners for the week and to work on the memory verse. Have each student write out the **Unit Memory Verse** and recite it to his or her partner.

Prayer
Bring the students back together and close in prayer.

2. Reason to Follow

Review

As you reflected on the cross you made, what did you learn about Jesus?

Did you find yourself doing anything differently during the week as a result?

In what ways were you encouraged or challenged?

Focus

During this meeting, you will discover two compelling reasons for following Jesus.

THE EXPERIENCE

Reason #1: We all have a spiritual thirst.

Read John 4:1–42 and learn about a woman who experienced a spiritual thirst.

. . . With Accountability

With your accountability partner, talk about your responses to the "Reflection" questions. Exchange phone numbers. Call each other this week to hold each other accountable to making an impact in your life.

name _____   phone _____

Review your memory verse by writing it out in the space below. Then recite it to your partner.

MEMORY VERSE
1 John 2:6

List three obstacles that might have prevented Jesus from even talking with this woman.

1.

2.

3.

How would you describe the Samaritan woman's thirst (or needs)?

What did Jesus offer to this woman?

Reason #2: Jesus is the Source that can fill our thirst.
What can you learn about Jesus from His encounter with the Samaritan woman?

What are some of the ways Jesus has chosen to fill our spiritual thirst?

What was most meaningful to you about our experience today?

What does God want you to do in response?

Summary Statements

We learned today that . . . .
- Everyone has a spiritual thirst.
- Jesus is the Source that can meet our thirst.

M A K E   A N   I M P A C T

. . . In Your Life
Let the cup you received serve as a reminder during the next week of why you follow Jesus. Every morning as you wake up, give your day to Jesus and commit to following Him and letting Him fill your needs. Every evening, before you go to sleep, write a word on the cup that represents how Jesus filled one of your needs during the day. It might be through an answered prayer, a special conversation, or experiencing Jesus' love and care through someone.

Has there ever been a time when Jesus offered you something that filled your thirst or need? Share it with your friends.

The Two-Step

Before the D-Team Experience

LEADER DEVOTION

"As Jesus started on his way, a man ran up to him and fell on his knees before him. 'Good teacher,' he asked, 'what must I do to inherit eternal life?' . . . Jesus looked at him and loved him. 'One thing you lack,' he said. 'Go, sell everything you have and give to the poor, and you will have treasure in heaven. Then come, follow me'" (Mark 10:17, 21).

Then come, follow me. A pretty big "then"! Jesus asked the man to sell everything because He knew this man's weakness—his love for money. If this man was ever going to be able to truly follow Jesus, he had to be able to make Jesus his Lord. Unfortunately, this "then" was just too big for the rich man. As you read the rest of the story, his feelings are clearly revealed: "At this the man's face fell. He went away sad, because he had great wealth" (v. 22). Riches and wealth were lord of this young man's life.

What about you? Would you be willing to give up something if God asked you to? Is He Lord over everything in your life, or are earthly possessions your major priority?

In preparation for this D-Team experience, take a moment to examine your weekly schedule. Then, list the priorities in your life. Are your priorities in sync with your schedule? Is Jesus Lord over everything in that schedule, or do you just try to "fit Him in"? As you prepare to lead, jot down your personal experiences and insights in the "Prep Notes" column so you can share them with the students. In your prayer time this week, ask for God's wisdom, discernment, and direction regarding the priorities in your life. *Then* make the adjustments you need to make and follow Him.

LOOKING AHEAD

Student Focus
Every D-Team member will discover how he or she can follow Jesus by taking two steps of obedience:

Step #1: Go to Jesus.
Step #2: *Then* make adjustments.

Unit Memory Verse
"Whoever claims to live in him must walk as Jesus did" (1 John 2:6).

Practical Impact
Your students will evaluate whether they are truly following Jesus by looking at their daily schedules and comparing them with the priorities in their lives. After this experience, you will challenge them to commit to the next three D-Team units so they can learn what it means to walk with Jesus.

BE PREPARED

Materials Needed
- Bibles and pens
- Duplicated Student Notes
- Student Contracts
- Inexpensive weekly planners for your students (Option 1)
- Clock (Option 1)

Special Preparation
- Review the Student Contract on page 32. You may photocopy it for your students or use it as a model for writing your own contract, incorporating the names of your student ministry and D-Teams.

Environment
To set up the environment for this D-Team experience, you can choose one of the following. Option 1 works in any setting; Option 2 moves the experience outside your normal setting.

Option 1: Begin this experience by writing out a typical weekly schedule. Provide each student with an inexpensive weekly planner. You may want to display a large clock in the room to emphasize the significance of a schedule.

Option 2: Since you will be studying the story of the rich young man, you may choose to meet in a place that represents wealth, like a conference room of a wealthy corporation or bank.

Leading the D-Team Experience
(60 min. total)

GET STARTED

Review
Ask your students to read the following from the "Review" section of the Student Notes: *Last week, you were challenged to let a cup be a reminder of why you follow Jesus. What did you learn about Jesus? Did you find yourself doing anything differently during the week as a result? In what ways were you encouraged or challenged?*

Focus
Share with your students that during this D-Team experience, they will discover how he or she can follow Jesus by taking two steps of obedience:

Step #1: Go to Jesus.
Step #2: *Then* **make adjustments.**

THE EXPERIENCE

Step #1: Go to Jesus.
Ask your students to use the space in the student notes to write down their schedules for a typical week. After they have finished, encourage them to share their schedules with each other. Put the schedules aside and begin the following study.

Have your D-Team members turn in their Bibles to Mark 10:17 to discover that the first step toward following Jesus is to go to Jesus.

Have a student *read aloud Mark 10:17–29.* Then discuss the following question: *Put yourself in the rich young man's shoes. He took the first step of going to Jesus by asking the question, "What must I do to inherit eternal life?" What kind of answer do you think he expected?* (Possible answers might include: "Don't worry, you've already got it"; "Keep doing all the good things you're doing"; "Give more money to the poor"; "Do more good things.")

Have students record Jesus' response to the young man in Mark 10:21. Ask them to underline the action words in the verse (*go, sell, give, come,* and *follow*). Also have them circle the word *Then.* Explain that after the rich man went to Jesus, Jesus told him exactly how to follow Him. The man was to take Step #2: *Then* make adjustments.

Step #2: *Then* make adjustments.
Jesus knew what the young man was thinking and feeling. Jesus told him to sell everything he owned and give the money to the poor, because Jesus knew the man's greatest weakness. Money was the idol or god he worshiped. The man was not following the first and greatest commandment: "Love the Lord your God with all your heart and with all your soul and with all your mind" (Matt. 22:37). Emphasize that the adjustments Jesus asked the man to make were adjustments that would allow Jesus to be Lord in his life.

Prep Notes

Ask your students to **read Mark 10:22–27 silently** to discover the man's response to Jesus. Then discuss the following question: **Why do you think the man responded this way?** (His riches were most important to him; Jesus asked for a sacrifice that was too great; he didn't realize who Jesus really was; he didn't know why it would be worth it to follow Jesus; he couldn't rely just on Jesus for his needs.)

Summarize that the man was not willing to make adjustments to give up his riches in return for the greatest gifts of all—a personal relationship with Jesus Christ and eternal life. The cost of sacrifice seemed too great compared to the benefits of following Jesus.

Have your students read Mark 10:21 and notice the *Then* that they circled. Explain that this *Then* seemed too big to the rich man. The man took Step #1 (go to Jesus) but Step #2 (*then* make adjustments) was too much. He could not follow Jesus and make Him Lord over everything.

Ask: **How does Jesus tell us what adjustments need to be made in our lives?** (Through the Bible, prayer, and wisdom from godly men and women.)

Ask your D-Team members: **Take a moment and list the five things that are most important in their lives. Then, number these things from most important to least important.** Encourage your students to be honest. If some students aren't ready to make Jesus Number One in their lives, they shouldn't feel pressured to write it down that way.

Then ask them to look at the weekly schedule they wrote down earlier. Ask: **Do your priorities match up with your schedule? Are you spending time on the things that are most important to you?**

 (5 min.)

REFLECTION

Share with your students that when we go to Jesus, He often asks us to make adjustments that allow Him to be Lord in our lives. Ask your students to reflect on the following questions: **When you go to Jesus, are there any adjustments He is asking you to make? Is Jesus Lord over everything in your life? Or do you just try to fit Him in a little bit here and a little bit there?**

Give your students a few moments to record honest responses to the following questions, found in their Student Notes: **What was most meaningful to you about our experience today? What does God want you to do in response?**

Ask a student to read aloud the Summary Statements in the Student Notes.

Summary Statements

We learned today that . . .
- To follow Jesus, we must first go to Jesus.
- After going to Jesus, *then* we can make adjustments in our priorities.

MAKE AN IMPACT

. . . In Your Life

Challenge your D-Team members to make one adjustment in their schedule this week. Possible adjustments might include:

- praying when they wake up;
- committing the day to Jesus;
- setting aside time to study the Bible;
- praying with a friend;
- cutting out TV or music that is not building them up.

Remind your students that the adjustment may involve a cost or sacrifice, just as it did for the rich young man, but taking the steps of choosing to follow Jesus will result in eternal benefits that will by far outweigh the costs.

After your students have chosen the adjustment they are going to make, ask them to consider making the adjustment of committing to the next nine student experiences so they can learn what it means to walk with Jesus.

Distribute the Student Contracts (p. XX) to your students. Discuss the expectations you have for them and the next three units. Don't make hollow promises of becoming best friends and hanging out every weekend; however, do encourage relationships to develop.

. . . With Accountability

Have the D-Team members form pairs to become accountability partners for the week and to work on the memory verse. Have each student write out the **Unit Memory Verse**, recite it to his or her partner, and share a way the verse is meaningful in his or her life.

Prayer

Bring the students back together and close in prayer.

Student Contract

I will cross the line . . .

. . . and lead a life of personal commitment to Jesus Christ, because I believe that together we will be only as strong as each member's personal commitment to Christ.

. . . and lead a life of integrity, because I believe the way I live my life shows people my commitment to Jesus Christ.

. . . and lead a life that makes a difference in the lives of other people, because I believe each of us needs to offer a hand back to someone else.

. . . and lead a life that is committed to attending my church and its student ministry, because I believe my participation in my church shows my commitment.

. . . and lead a life that is committed to attending and participating in my student ministry, because I believe my participation in my student ministry shows my commitment.

. . . and lead a life that is committed to prayer, because I believe my prayers make a difference.

. . . and pray that one day I may be a student ministry leader, because I believe I can give back to other people what God has given to me through my student ministry.

Signed: _____ Date: _____

3. The Two-Step

Review

Last week, you were challenged to let a cup be a reminder of why you follow Jesus. What did you learn about Jesus? Did you find yourself doing anything differently during the week as a result? In what ways were you encouraged or challenged?

Focus

During this experience, you will discover how to follow Jesus by taking two steps of obedience.

THE EXPERIENCE

Step #1: Go to Jesus.
Write down your schedule for a typical week.

	M	T	W	T	F	S	S
8 AM							
9 AM							
10 AM							
11 AM							
12 PM							
1 PM							
2 PM							
3 PM							
4 PM							
5 PM							
6 PM							
7 PM							
8 PM							

MAKE AN IMPACT

... In Your Life
Consider making one adjustment in your schedule this week. Possible adjustments might include: praying when you wake up; committing the day to Jesus; setting aside time to study the Bible; praying with a friend; cutting out TV or music that is not building you up. Record the adjustment that you will make in the space below:

Now consider making the adjustment of committing to the next nine student experiences so you can learn what it means to walk with Jesus.

... With Accountability
With your accountability partner, talk about your responses to the "Reflection" questions. Exchange phone numbers. Call each other this week to hold each other accountable to making an impact in your life.

name

phone

Review your memory verse by writing it out in the space below. After reciting it to your partner, share a way the verse is meaningful in your life.

MEMORY VERSE
1 John 2:6

Read Mark 10:17–29. Put yourself in the rich young man's shoes. He took the first step of going to Jesus by asking the question, "What must I do to inherit eternal life?" What kind of answer do you think he expected?

In the space below, record Jesus' response to the young man in Mark 10:21. Underline the action words in the verse. Then circle the word *Then*.

Step #2: Then make adjustments.
Silently read Mark 10:22–27 to discover the man's response to Jesus. Why do you think the man responded this way?

How does Jesus tell us what adjustments need to be made in our lives?

Take a moment and list the five things that are most important in your life (from most important to least important).

1.

2.

3.

4.

5.

Now look at the weekly schedule you wrote down earlier. Do your priorities match up with your schedule? How can you spend more time on the things that are most important to you?

R E F L E C T I O N

When you go to Jesus, are there any adjustments He is asking you to make? Is Jesus Lord over everything in your life? Or do you just try to fit Him in a little bit here and a little bit there?

What was most meaningful to you about our experience today?

What does God want you to do in response?

Summary Statements

We learned today that . . .
- To follow Jesus, we must first go to Jesus.
- After going to Jesus, *then* we can make adjustments in our priorities.

LEADER FOCUS

What is the first thought that comes to mind when you hear the word *love*? Is it a memory from the past? A person? An event in your life that brings up feelings of love? Reflect on what God intends for us to associate with the word *love*. He created us to have a relationship with Him based on love. Take the next few moments to write a love letter to your Creator, your Savior, and your King—Jesus. Just hearing His name should bring the thought of pure love to your mind.

BIG PICTURE

Unit Overview
In Unit 2 we will be focusing on learning how to live a life of love by answering three questions: (1) What is love? (2) Why love God? (3) How can I love God?

1. Love of Another Kind
During this D-Team experience, your students will practice biblical love by taking two simple steps:

> Step #1: Identify the difference between the world's view of love and God's view of love.
> Step #2: Identify what aspect of love we most need to develop.

2. Rescue 911
During this D-Team experience, your students will identify two reasons why we should be motivated to love God:

> Reason #1: We should love God because He has paid for our sins.
> Reason #2: We should love God because He commands us to love Him.

3. Express Your Love
During this D-Team experience, your students will be able to express love to God by practicing two crucial skills:

> Skill #1: Get to know who Jesus is by reading God's Word.
> Skill #2: Take time to talk to God through prayer.

Unit 2 Introduction

Unit Memory Verse
"Be imitators of God, therefore, as dearly loved children and live a life of love, just as Christ loved us and gave himself up for us as a fragrant offering and sacrifice to God" (Eph. 5:1–2).

Love of Another Kind

Before the D-Team Experience

LEADER DEVOTION

Take time to write out 1 Corinthians 13:1–7, substituting your name for the word *I*. Now read it aloud until you really hear it. Is there anything that the Holy Spirit is gently pointing out to you regarding the way that you love? Allow Jesus to help you change and be different today and tomorrow and the day after that.

As you prepare to lead the meeting, jot down your personal experiences and insights in the "Prep Notes" column so you can share them with the students. Don't miss the opportunity to be transparent with your D-Team members regarding whatever aspect of biblical love you are working on. Otherwise, they may not have a role model who proves the validity of this week's study.

Take a moment to thank God for giving us 1 Corinthians 13 as a guideline for loving. Ask God to help you take to heart the truths you will teach your students.

LOOKING AHEAD

Student Focus
Every D-Team member will discover how to practice biblical love by taking two simple steps:

Step #1:   Identify the difference between the world's view of love and God's view of love.
Step #2:   Identify what aspect of love we most need to develop.

Unit Memory Verse
"Be imitators of God, therefore, as dearly loved children and live a life of love, just as Christ loved us and gave himself up for us as a fragrant offering and sacrifice to God" (Eph. 5:1–2).

Practical Impact
Your students will discover how they can live lives of love by answering the question: "What is love?"

GETTING READY

Materials Needed
- Bibles and pens
- Duplicated Student Notes
- Personal tokens of love (Option A; see "Special Preparation")
- Scissors, teen magazines (Option B)
- *TV Guides*, movie guides, music magazines (Option C)

Special Preparation

Contact your D-Team members and ask them to bring tokens of love to the meeting. Such items might include jewelry, dried flowers, valentine cards, prom pictures, etc. Ask them to be prepared to share when, where, and why they received them.

Environment

To set up the environment for this D-Team experience, you can choose one of the following. Option 1 works in any setting; Option 2 moves the experience outside your normal setting.

Option 1: Since you will be studying 1 Corinthians 13 (the "love chapter" of the Bible), decorate your meeting area with some tokens of love.

Option 2: Have your D-Team meet in a place where you might normally see a lot of love displayed from the world's perspective—outside of a movie theater, in a small, quiet cafe, or in someone's home. Meet there to provide atmosphere and spur creativity.

Leading the D-Team Experience
(60 min. total)

GET STARTED

Unit Preview
Have a student read aloud the following information from the "Preview" in the Student Notes: **As you work together through "Unit 2: What's Love Got to Do with It?" you will discover how to live a life of love by answering three questions:**
1. **What is love?**
2. **Why love God?**
3. **How can I love God?**

Unit Memory Verse
Read aloud Ephesians 5:1–2, "Be imitators of God, therefore, as dearly loved children and live a life of love, just as Christ loved us and gave himself up for us as a fragrant offering and sacrifice to God," explaining that the sacrificial way Jesus expressed His love for us on the cross is not only the means of salvation, but also an example of how we are to live.

Student Prayer
Ask a volunteer to pray for a time of growth and understanding of the meaning of love.

Focus
Share with your D-Team members that they will discover how to practice biblical love by taking two simple steps:

> **Step #1: Identify the difference between the world's view of love and God's view of love.**
> **Step #2: Identify what aspect of love we most need to develop.**

THE EXPERIENCE

Step #1: Identify the difference between the world's view of love and God's view of love.
Begin by asking your D-Team members: **What is your definition of the word** love. Then ask: **What does "being in love" look like?**

Choose one of the following options that best fits your D-Team members.

Option A
Have your students share their tokens of love—when, where, and why they received them. Then ask volunteers to explain how people use these items to show love.

Option B
Supply your D-Team members with magazines and scissors. Ask them to cut out pictures, phrases, and/or words they think represent the world's definition of *love*.

Option C
Have your D-Team members look through *TV Guide*, movie guides, and music magazines, and list movies, songs, and TV shows that focus on love. Then discuss what the world says love is.

Prep Notes

After you've completed one of the options, ask your D-Team members: **Complete the first column of the chart in your Student Notes.** Tell them to draw from the ideas they came up with in the previous activity to describe how the world defines love.

Have a student **read 1 Corinthians 13:4–7 aloud.** Then ask your students to **start naming what God says love is, filling in God's perspective of love on the chart.**

After your students have filled out both perspectives, compare and discuss the differences. Ask: **Which perspective would you want others (parents, friends, etc.) to love you with?**

Step #2: Identify what aspect of love we most need to develop.
Challenge your D-Team members by saying, "What does love have to do with this relationship between Christ and you? Everything! First Corinthians 13 is not just a chapter of instructions on how God wants us to love others. He commands us to love Him first. How? First Corinthians 13 is a perfect guideline."

Have your D-Team members write their names in all the blanks in the following verses from 1 Corinthians 13. Then ask them to silently read the following paragraph:

"_____ is patient, _____ is kind. _____ does not envy, _____ does not boast, _____ is not proud. _____ is not rude, _____ is not self-seeking, _____ is not easily angered, _____ keeps no record of wrongs. _____ does not delight in evil but rejoices with the truth. _____ always protects, always trusts, always hopes, always perseveres. Love never fails" (1 Cor. 13:4–8a).

Discuss the following questions: **Which of the above statements do you have a hard time saying honestly? Which statement/quality is something you would admit that you need to work on? Circle it.**

🕐 **(5 min.)**

REFLECTION

Remind your students of the two steps to practicing biblical love. First, they identified the difference between the world's love and God's love. Second, they applied 1 Corinthians 13 to their own lives and determined what aspect they needed to work on.

Have your students determine a practical way to change in the area they circled earlier.

Share with your students that none of these actions is easy to master by ourselves, but we have the Holy Spirit inside of us to encourage and help us. When we express any of these qualities, we are expressing our love toward God. With that kind of love inside our hearts, we will in turn love others more naturally, because God will love others through us.

Give your students a few moments to record honest responses to the following questions, found in their Student Notes: **What was most meaningful to you about our experience today? What does God want you to do in response?**

Ask a student to read aloud the Summary Statements in the Student Notes.

Summary Statements

We learned today that . . .
- We can practice biblical love by distinguishing the difference between worldly love and godly love.
- We can practice biblical love by following the example given in 1 Corinthians 13.

MAKE AN IMPACT

. . . In Your Life
Ask your D-Team members if, during this week, they would like to make a commitment to work on the specific aspect of love they circled earlier. Suggest that they take their Student Notes (particularly the segment where they wrote their names in 1 Corinthians 13), and put them where they will see them everyday. Throughout the week, as they see opportunities to love God the way He intended, they need to take the challenge to be different. Others will see their love for God and be attracted to a different kind of love than what the world has to offer.

. . . With Accountability
Have students form pairs to become accountability partners for the week and to work on the memory verse. Have each student begin learning the **Unit Memory Verse** by writing it out in the space provided in the Student Notes.

Prayer
Bring the students back together and close in prayer.

1. Love of Another Kind

Preview

As you work together through "Unit 2: What's Love Got to Do with It?" you will discover how to live a life of love by answering three questions:

1. What is love?
2. Why love God?
3. How can I love God?

Unit Memory Verse

"Be imitators of God, therefore, as dearly loved children and live a life of love, just as Christ loved us and gave himself up for us as a fragrant offering and sacrifice to God" (Eph. 5:1–2).

Focus

During this meeting, you will discover how to take two steps to practice biblical love.

THE EXPERIENCE

Step #1: Identify the difference between the world's view of love and God's view of love.

What is your definition of love? What does "being in love" look like?

MAKE AN IMPACT

. . . In Your Life

During this next week, would you like to make a commitment to work on the specific aspect of love that you circled earlier? If so, take your Student Notes and put them where you will see them every day. Throughout the week, as you see opportunities to love God the way He intended, you need to take the challenge to be different. Others will see your love for God and be attracted to a different kind of love than what the world has to offer.

. . . With Accountability

With your accountability partner, talk about your responses to the "Reflection" questions. Exchange phone numbers. Call each other this week to hold each other accountable to making an impact in your life.

name _____ phone _____

Begin learning your memory verse by writing it out in the space below.

MEMORY VERSE
Ephesians 5:1–2

Record the world's perspective of love on the chart below.

WORLD'S PERSPECTIVE OF LOVE	GOD'S PERSPECTIVE OF LOVE (1 Corinthians 13)

Read 1 Corinthians 13:4–7. Now record God's perspective of love on the chart. After you have filled out both perspectives, compare and discuss the differences.

Which perspective would you want others (parents, friends, etc.) to love you with?

Step #2: Identify what aspect of love we most need to develop. In 1 Corinthians 13, we find the perfect instructions on how God wants us to love Him and others. Write your name in all the blanks in the following verses from 1 Corinthians 13. Then silently read the paragraph.

"_____ is patient, _____ is kind. _____ does not envy, _____ does not boast, _____ is not proud. _____ is not rude, _____ is not self-seeking, _____ is not easily angered, _____ keeps no record of wrongs. _____ does not delight in evil but rejoices with the truth. _____ always protects, always trusts, always hopes, always perseveres. Love never fails" (1 Cor. 13:4–8a).

Which of the above statements do you have a hard time saying honestly?

Which statement/quality is something you would admit that you need to work on? Circle it.

R E F L E C T I O N

During this meeting, you have taken two steps to practicing biblical love. First, you identified the difference between the world's love and God's love. Second, you applied 1 Corinthians 13 to your own life and determined what aspect you needed to work on.

What was most meaningful to you about our experience today?

What does God want you to do in response?

Summary Statements

We learned today that . . .
- We can practice biblical love by distinguishing the difference between worldly love and godly love.
- We can practice biblical love by following the example given in 1 Corinthians 13.

Rescue 911

Before the D-Team Experience

LEADER DEVOTION

When was the last time you were rescued from a near-death experience? Can't remember? Read Mark 15:21–16:7. Now answer that question again. Take some time to refresh your memory and recall why you love Jesus. Your challenge this week is to prepare yourself to be used by God. As you prepare to lead the meeting, jot down your personal experiences and insights in the "Prep Notes" column so you can share them with the students. Don't miss the opportunity to be transparent with your students about why you love God. Your transparency and vulnerability will have a lasting effect on your students' faith.

LOOKING AHEAD

Student Focus
During this D-Team experience, your students will be able to identify two reasons why we should be motivated to love God:

Reason #1: We should love God because He has paid for our sins.
Reason #2: We should love God because He commands us to love Him.

Unit Memory Verse
"Be imitators of God, therefore, as dearly loved children and live a life of love, just as Christ loved us and gave himself up for us as a fragrant offering and sacrifice to God" (Eph. 5:1–2).

Practical Impact
During this D-Team, your students will watch a video of a TV show such as *Rescue 911* in order to illustrate life-saving situations. You will have a chance to illustrate one of the motivations to love God as you compare those situations with the saving of lives that Jesus did on the cross.

BE PREPARED

Materials Needed
- Bibles and pens
- Duplicated Student Notes
- TV and VCR (Option 1)
- A token "911" symbol for each student (piece of wood, tag board, red paper, emergency patch, etc.)

Special Preparation
- Record a TV show such as *Cops* or *Rescue 911*. You will need a segment that displays someone saving a person's life. Try to make sure you tape the part where the rescued person thanks his or her rescuer.

• Write "911" on whatever symbol your have chosen for your students.

Environment

To set up the environment for this D-Team experience, you can choose one of the following. Option 1 works in any setting; Option 2 moves the experience outside your normal setting.

Option 1: Set up a TV and VCR in your meeting area. Try to create the atmosphere of an emergency room or police/fire station with banners, alarms, or a gurney. You might borrow a nursing uniform or surgeon's "greens" from medical personnel.

Option 2: Meet at a student's house who has a TV and VCR. After watching the prerecorded video, have your group visit an emergency room or police/fire station to capture the atmosphere of a life-saving situation.

Leading the D-Team Experience

(60 min. total)

GET STARTED

Review

Have a student read aloud the information under "Review" in the Student Notes: **Last week you were challenged to work on an aspect of love from 1 Corinthians 13. If you took the challenge, how are you different as a result?**

Student Prayer

Ask a volunteer to pray that this D-Team meeting will be a time of growth and understanding of why we should love God.

Focus

Share with your group that during this D-Team experience they will be able to identify two reasons why we should be motivated to love God:

Reason #1: We should love God because He has paid for our sins.
Reason #2: We should love God because He commands us to love Him.

THE EXPERIENCE

Begin your D-Team by asking if anyone has ever watched the show *Rescue 911*. Then ask: **Have you ever been in a situation where you needed someone to save your life or rescue you? How did you feel toward the one who rescued you?**

Now have your students view the prerecorded video segment and discuss the following questions. If you are not able to show a segment of the show, then create a hypothetical situation and discuss the following questions that seem appropriate: **Would the person who was in trouble have lived without the help from the other person? How did that person help? What would you have done if you were the person needing help? What would you have done to help someone in the same situation? What would your reaction have been to the person who helped you when you got to meet him or her again? What would you say to that person? Would you want to keep in touch with that person? Why or why not?**

Reason #1: We should love God because He has paid for our sins.

Have your students take a look at some people in the Bible who were desperately in need and who had someone call "911" for them. Have each of the students look up the passages listed on the chart and fill in the columns, then briefly share what they learned.

PASSAGE	PERSON/SITUATION	JESUS' RESPONSE	PERSON'S RESPONSE
Luke 13: 10–13	crippled woman	Jesus healed her.	She praised God!
Luke 18: 35–43	blind beggar	Jesus made him see.	The man followed Jesus praising Him, and when the crowd saw it, they also praised God!

PASSAGE	PERSON/SITUATION	JESUS' RESPONSE	PERSON'S RESPONSE
John 4: 46–53	*official whose son was dying*	*Jesus healed his son long-distance.*	*The father and all his household believed!*
John 9: 1–7, 14–17 35b–38	*man born blind*	*Jesus made him see.*	*The blind man believed Jesus is the Son of God and worshiped Him!*

All of these people were touched by Jesus and healed, which is awesome! Now have your students look up Mark 17:1–10.

After students have looked in their Bibles, say, "Obviously, there is not a Chapter 17 in Mark. But if there were, would it include your "911" story?" Take a moment to hand out the symbol with "911" on it that you made for your D-Team members. Or have your students write the "911" on the object right now.

Have your students take a brief look at **Mark 15:21–16:7.** What a moving episode of *Rescue 911* this story would make! **What motivation does this give you for loving God?** (He has rescued us from sin.)

Jesus hasn't just offered to touch and heal us. In fact, He got our "911" before we even realized that we needed help. His Father informed Him that the only way to save us would be to give up His life so that we would have a chance to live. The passage in Mark is in fact *our* "911" story!

Ask your students to recall how the people in the video got to meet the person who rescued them. Ask: **If you were able to meet face to face with Jesus, what would you say to Him?**

Summarize by asking your students what is the first reason why they should love God. Point out that after hearing what God has done for them, how can they *not* love Him?

Reason #2: We should love God because He commands us to love Him.
Share with your students that there is another reason why we should love God. Have volunteers **read Mark 12:28–30.** Ask: **What is the second reason for loving God?** Note that it's not a suggestion or advice, it is an order from the King Himself. We must obey.

 (5 min.)

REFLECTION

Remind your students of the two reasons to love God. How did this experience affect your desire to love God? Note that when we experience the first reason we should love God, we will be motivated to be obedient to God's command to love Him.

Give your students a few moments to record honest responses to the following questions, found in their Student Notes: **What was most meaningful to you about our experience today? What does God want you to do in response?**

Ask a student to read aloud the Summary Statements in the Student Notes.

Summary Statements
We learned today that . . . • We should be motivated to love God because of what Jesus did on the cross for us. • We are commanded by God to love Him.

MAKE AN IMPACT

(10 min.)

. . . In Your Life

Suggest that your students carry their "911" symbols with them this week to remind them of the response Jesus has given to our emergency call. The next time they see someone in need or find themselves in need, they can be reminded of the ultimate sacrifice God has made.

. . . With Accountability

Have the D-Team members form pairs to become accountability partners for the week and to work on the memory verse. Have each student write out the **Unit Memory Verse** and recite it to his or her partner.

Prayer

Bring the students back together and close in prayer.

2. Rescue 911!

Review
Last week, you were challenged to work on an aspect of love from 1 Corinthians 13. If you took the challenge, how are you different as a result?

Focus
This week, you will be able to identify two reasons why we should be motivated to love God.

THE EXPERIENCE

Have you ever been in a situation where you needed someone to save your life or rescue you? How did you feel toward the one who saved your life?

Answer these questions after watching the video segment:

Would the person who was in trouble have lived without the help from the other person?

How did that person help?

What would you have done if you were the person needing help?

What would you have done to help someone in the same situation?

MAKE AN IMPACT

. . . In Your Life
Plan to carry your "911" symbol with you this week to remind you of the response Jesus has given to our emergency call. The next time you see someone in need or find yourself in need, you can remember the ultimate sacrifice God has made.

. . . With Accountability
With your accountability partner, talk about your responses to the "Reflection" questions. Exchange phone numbers. Call each other this week to hold each other accountable to making an impact in your life.

name _____ phone _____

Review your memory verse by writing it out in the space below. Then recite it to your partner.

MEMORY VERSE
Ephesians 5:1–2

What would your reaction have been to the person who helped you when you got to meet him or her again? What would you say to that person?

Would you want to keep in touch with that person? Why or why not?

Reason #1: We should love God because He has died for our sins.
Take a look at some people in the Bible who were desperately in need and who had someone call "911" for them.

PASSAGE	PERSON/SITUATION	JESUS' RESPONSE	PERSON'S RESPONSE
Luke 13: 10–13			
Luke 18: 35–43			
John 4: 46–53			
John 9: 1–7, 14–17, 35b–38			

Read Mark 15:21–16:7. What motivation does this give you for loving God?

If you were able to meet face to face with Jesus, what would you say to Him?

Reason #2: We should love God because He commands us to love Him.
Read Mark 12:28–30. What is the second reason for loving God?

R E F L E C T I O N

Rather than beginning this experience by saying we should love God because He has commanded us to do so, we examined what Jesus has done for us. How did this experience affect your desire to love God?

What was most meaningful to you about our experience today?

What does God want you to do in response?

Summary Statements

- We should be motivated to love God because of what Jesus did on the cross for us.
- We are commanded by God to love Him.

Express Your Love!

Before the D-Team Experience

LEADER DEVOTION

Who do you love the most in this world? What is the best way to show that person that you love him or her? Do you tell the person? Hug him or her? Give a gift? Send a card? Sing it? Write a poem? Plan a surprise? Spend quality time with the person? Include the loved one in everything? Share secrets? Remember and be sensitive to the person's likes and dislikes?

How do you express love and devotion to your Lord and Savior, Jesus? In one or all the ways listed above? If not, maybe all you need are some suggestions.

Don't rush through this because you want to get going on the study for your students. If you can't remember the last time you displayed affection toward your Lord, your love relationship with Jesus is lacking and your students will know it. Ask yourself when and why you stopped expressing your love, and how you can begin expressing it now. Before you move on, try expressing your love to Jesus through one of the suggestions listed above.

As you prepare to lead the meeting, jot down your personal experiences and insights in the "Prep Notes" column so you can share them with your students.

LOOKING AHEAD

Student Focus
During this D-Team experience, your students will be able to express love to God by practicing two crucial skills:

Skill #1: Get to know who Jesus is by reading God's Word.
Skill #2: Take time to talk to God through prayer.

Unit Memory Verse
"Be imitators of God, therefore, as dearly loved children and live a life of love, just as Christ loved us and gave himself up for us as a fragrant offering and sacrifice to God" (Eph. 5:1–2).

Practical Impact
At the end of the meeting, students will make grab bags of creative ideas to use this week during their personal devotions.

BE PREPARED

Materials Needed
- Bibles and pens
- Duplicated Student Notes
- Pots, pans, spoons, or any objects in which you can see your reflection
- A mirror for each student
- Small paper bags and strips of paper

- Worship music (Option 1)
- Copies of *A Love Letter from Jesus* for your students (see "Special Preparation")

Special Preparation
Type or handwrite the following letter for each of your students.

A Love Letter from Jesus
Dear child,

I want you to know Me.

I want you to rely on Me.

I want you to trust Me.

I want you to love Me.

I created you—I won't ever reject you because of a weakness or mistake.

You are My child. I know the number of hairs on your head!

I want you to share your hurts with Me so I can comfort you.

I want you to share your accomplishments with Me, so I can celebrate with you.

I want you to share your dreams with Me, so I can help you reach them.

I want you to share your fears with Me, so I can protect you and help you conquer them.

I want you to ask Me for things, so I can give you what would be best for you.

I love you, child. I want you to find happiness and contentment through Me.

I will give you a peace that no one will be able to understand or explain.

Turn toward Me. I'm waiting.

Lovingly,

Jesus

Environment
To set up the environment for this D-Team experience, you can choose one of the following. Option 1 works in any setting; Option 2 moves the experience outside your normal setting.

Option 1: Create a quiet atmosphere within your meeting area by softening the lighting. You could also have worship music playing as your students arrive. Have your students sit on the floor to give a more relaxed feeling.

Option 2: Meet in a quiet, secluded place (a lake or park) to illustrate the necessity of having quality time with God.

Leading the D-Team Experience
(60 min. total)

GET STARTED

Review

Have a student read aloud the information under "Review" in the Student Notes: **Last week you answered the question: "Why love God?" What are the two reasons we should love God with our whole hearts? How did carrying your "911" symbol last week remind you of Jesus' love?**

Student Prayer
Ask a student to pray that God will teach each D-Team member about talking to Him.

Focus
Share with your students that during this D-Team experience they will be able to express love to God by practicing two crucial skills:

Skill #1: Get to know who Jesus is by reading God's Word.
Skill #2: Take time to talk to God through prayer.

THE EXPERIENCE

(40 min.)

Ask your students: **Who do you love the most on this earth?** Have them complete the checklist found in their Student Notes of ways to show love to that person. Say, "What is the best way that someone can show love to you? If someone pursued you, calling you daily, asking you to do things and go places, would you feel loved and cared for?"

Allow plenty of time for students to share. Then explain that we will learn how to show or express our love to God during this D-Team meeting.

Have your students **read 1 Corinthians 8:3.** Ask: **What does this verse mean?** As most of your students have probably determined by now whether they love God, the beginning of that verse is answered. Now discuss the meaning of the second half of the verse: "is known by God." Explain that the verse is the picture of a two-way relationship.

Have your students recall the person they mentioned at the beginning of the meeting. Then ask them to answer a few more questions about their relationship with the person they mentioned.

How often do you talk to the person?

How often do you spend time together?

Do you feel as if you know a lot about the person? Do you know more than most other people know about the person?

Does this person know a lot about you?

Prep Notes

Does this person know things about you that you wouldn't tell most other people?

Would you call this person a close friend? Why or why not?

Now have your students answer those same questions in regard to their relationship with God.

How often do you talk to God?

How often do you spend time with Him?

Do you feel as if you know a lot about God? Do you know more than most other people know about Him?

Does God know a lot about you?

Does He know things about you that you wouldn't tell most other people?

Would you call God a close friend? Why or why not?

Hand out spoons, pots, or pans (any objects in which you can see a reflection) to each of your students. Tell them to look into the objects and notice how clearly they can see themselves.

What if we couldn't see our loved ones face to face? What if the reflections in these objects were the only reflections we could see? If we couldn't see our loved ones face to face, wouldn't we work harder to get the best possible vision or reflection available?

In her book *Living Love* (Harold Shaw, 1993), author Jill Briscoe says that people in Paul's day didn't have glass mirrors. They only had pieces of highly polished bronze or copper. When they looked in it, they saw an imperfect reflection. Ask your students to imagine Paul carrying a small pocket-size piece of bronze. When he looked into it, he saw a poor reflection of himself. Poor Paul never knew what he looked like! No wonder Paul used that parallel to talk about seeing God. Explain that we may not be able to see God face to face until we reach heaven, but we *can* get a better "mirrored" reflection.

Distribute mirrors to your students. Ask them whether they would rather see the person they love in the first object you gave them, or in the mirror. Why?

Tell the students that we can choose to see God through a distorted reflection, or we can see Him more clearly every day by practicing two crucial skills—the same skills we use to pursue a friendship with someone here on earth.

Skill #1: Get to know who Jesus is by reading God's Word.
First, we need to get to know who Jesus is. How? His story, personality, and power are beautifully written in His Book—the Bible. *Take a look at the following passages and note anything new you discover about Jesus.*

John 1:1–2, 14—Emphasize that Jesus is God in the fullest sense; He existed before the creation of humankind; He gives spiritual illumination; He is filled with grace and truth.

John 20:26–31—Point out that Jesus rose from the dead and appeared to His disciples; He is the Son of God; He is able to give us life.

Skill #2: Take time to talk to God through prayer.
We also need to take time to talk to God through prayer. He wants to hear our voices. It's like making a phone call every day, but it doesn't cost us anything except time!

Say: ***Take a look at the following passages that tell us how to pray.***

Hebrews 4:14–16—Point out that we have a High Priest who is sympathetic to our prayers and is ready to give us help.

Matthew 6:5–13—Explain that the Lord's Prayer is more a picture of what should be included in a prayer, rather than the exact words to be spoken.

Do you believe God wants to know you intimately? God created the first man and woman so that He could have a personal relationship with them. He walked and talked with them daily until they sinned. Then, because of sin, there was a separation. But Jesus died on the cross and rose again, wiping our slates clean. Now we can have an intimate personal relationship with the God of the universe. He created us from the beginning, to have a continuing friendship with Him. He's ready. We just have to make the effort from our side. He wants to hear what is going on in our lives—the joys, the hurts, the laughter, the worries—all of it!

REFLECTION

(5 min.)

We all probably have known people who say they want to be our friends or call us their good friend, but we don't talk to them or do anything with them. They eventually fade out of our lives. Don't make that mistake with the best friend you could ever have!

Ask your students to think about what kind of difference it would make in their life to invest in a friendship with God. Encourage them to show God their love by spending time with Him daily, using the two skills they learned today.

Give your students a few moments to record honest responses to the following questions, found in their Student Notes: ***What was most meaningful to you about our experience today? What does God want you to do in response?***

Ask a student to read aloud the Summary Statements in the Student Notes.

Summary Statements

We learned today that . . .
- We can express our love to God by getting to know Jesus through reading His Word.
- We can express our love to God by taking time to talk to Him through prayer.

MAKE AN IMPACT

(10 min.)

. . . In Your Life
Distribute small paper bags and slips of paper. Have your students brainstorm some suggestions for different ways to show love to God during the next week. Then have them record their suggestions on the slips of paper. During the week, when they take ten minutes to practice their skills for expressing love, they can choose one of the

slips of paper in their bag. Suggestions might include to sing a song, write a letter, write a poem, play a worship song, rewrite a psalm, or do a short Bible study.

.. With Accountability

Have the D-Team members form pairs to become accountability partners for the week and to work on the memory verse. Have each student write out the **Unit Memory Verse**, recite it to his or her partner, and share a way the verse is meaningful in his or her life.

Prayer

Bring your students back together. Distribute copies of *A Love Letter from Jesus* and ask your students to read it silently. Close in prayer.

3. Express Your Love!

Review

Last week you answered the question: "Why love God?" What are the two reasons we should love God with our whole hearts? How did carrying your "911" symbol last week remind you of Jesus' love?

Focus

This week, you will be able to express love to God by practicing two crucial skills.

THE EXPERIENCE

Who do you love the most on this earth? What is the best way to show that person that you love him or her? Check all that apply:

— Tell the person that you love him or her.
— Hug the person.
— Give gifts.
— Send a card.
— Sing it.
— Write a poem.
— Surprise the person.
— Spend quality time with the person.
— Include the person in everything.
— Share secrets.
— Remember and be sensitive to the person's likes and dislikes.

Read 1 Corinthians 8:3. What does this verse mean?

Answer the following questions about your relationship with the person you mentioned earlier:

How often do you talk to the person?

MAKE AN IMPACT

. . . In Your Life

Record your friends' suggestions for different ways to show love to God on the slips of paper provided. During the week, when you take ten minutes to practice your skills for expressing love, choose one of the slips of paper in your bag. Be creative! God made you, so He will enjoy whatever you come up with!

. . . With Accountability

With your accountability partner, talk about your responses to the "Reflection" questions. Exchange phone numbers. Call each other this week to hold each other accountable to making an impact in your life.

name

phone

Review your memory verse by writing it out in the space below. After reciting it to your partner, share a way the verse is meaningful in your life.

MEMORY VERSE
Ephesians 5:1–2

How often do you spend time together?

Do you feel as if you know a lot about the person? Do you know more than most other people know about the person?

Does this person know things about you?

Does this person know a lot about you?

Would you call this person a close friend? Why or why not?

Now answer those same questions in regard to your relationship with God:

How often do you spend time with Him?

How often do you talk to God?

Does God know a lot about you?

Do you feel as if you know a lot about God? Do you know more than most other people know about Him?

Does He know things about you that you wouldn't tell most other people?

Would you call God a close friend? Why or why not?

Skill #1: Get to know who Jesus is by reading God's Word.
Take a look at the following passages and note anything new you discover about Jesus:

John 1:1-2, 14—

John 20:26-31—

Skill #2: Take time to talk to God through prayer.
Take a look at the following passages that tell us how to pray:

Hebrews 4:14-16—

Matthew 6:5-13—

R E F L E C T I O N

What difference would it make in your life to invest in a friendship with the God who created you? Consider showing God you love Him by spending time with Him daily! Try using the two skills you learned today by reading beginning to take ten minutes daily to read His Word and pray.

What was most meaningful to you about our experience today?

What does God want you to do in response?

Summary Statements

We learned today that . . .
- We can express our love to God by getting to know Jesus through reading His Word.
- We can express our love to God by taking time to talk to Him through prayer.

STUDENT IMPACT

LEADER FOCUS

Have you ever read Hebrews 11? What a hall of fame . . . or perhaps we should say a hall of faith! Take the time to read this entire chapter of Hebrews. Note each character who had faith and what area of their lives they entrusted to God. Was there anything extraordinary about these people? Ask yourself, *Would I have had faith in that situation?* What is Jesus asking you to trust Him with today? May your faith of a mustard seed move mountains for you.

BIG PICTURE

Unit Overview
In Unit 3 we will be focusing on learning how to walk by faith by answering three questions: (1) What is faith? (2) Why have faith? (3) How do I live by faith?

1. Faith Equations
During this D-Team experience, your students will discover what faith is by understanding two essential factors of faith:

Faith Factor #1: Trust
Faith Factor #2: Action

2. Faith Builders
During this D-Team experience, your students will have an opportunity to be assured of God's faithfulness by practicing two faith builders:

Faith Builder #1: Know God's promises.
Faith Builder #2: Remember God's faithfulness.

3. Faith in Action
During this D-Team experience, your students will discover how to live by faith by taking two action steps:

Action Step #1: Stand Up.
Action Step #2: Look to Jesus.

Unit Memory Verse
"In the same way, faith by itself, if it is not accompanied by action, is dead" (James 2:17).

Faith Equation

Before the D-Team Experience

Men and women through faith have . . . conquered kingdoms, administered justice, gained what was promised, shut the mouths of lions, quenched the fury of the flames, escaped the edge of the sword, experienced weakness turned to strength (adapted from Heb. 11).

There is no doubt that God has done incredible things through men and women of faith. Faith is a command, a defensive weapon ("shield of faith"), indispensable, essential in prayer, and blessed. And yet, faith often confuses us. *How much or how little do I need? If I have more faith, will this happen? How do I get more?*

Even the disciples cried out for help to the Lord, "Increase our faith," they cried (Luke 17:5). Read the story of the Roman centurion's faith in Matthew 8:5–13. Would you have had faith similar to the centurion's, or would you have been filled with doubts and fears? Pray that, as you prepare for this D-Team experience, Christ will reveal truths to you about your faith. As you prepare to lead, jot down your personal experiences and insights in the "Prep Notes" column so you can share them with your students.

LOOKING AHEAD

Student Focus
Every D-Team member will discover what faith is by understanding two essential factors of faith:

    Faith Factor #1: Trust
    Faith Factor #2: Action

Unit Memory Verse
"In the same way, faith by itself, if it is not accompanied by action, is dead" (James 2:17).

Practical Impact
Students will take home a mustard seed and reflect during the week on what it means to trust God's promise in Matthew 17:20 to move the "mountains" in their lives.

BE PREPARED

Materials Needed
- Bibles and pens
- Duplicated Student Notes
- A dictionary and a concordance
- A clothespin and a mustard seed for each student
- Blindfolds for half of your students (Option B)

Special Preparation

Before your D-Team experience, write the Bible reference (Matt. 17:20) on each clothespin.

Environment

To set up the environment for this D-Team experience, you can choose one of the following. Option 1 works in any setting; Option 2 moves the experience outside your normal setting.

Option 1: Create an environment of trust by starting your D-Team experience wtih either a trust fall or a trust walk.

Option 2: Since you will be examining the meaning of faith, you may want to have your D-Team members meet at a church, Christian college, or other building that exists as a result of a person's faith. Be sure to share the founder's story of faith in action.

Prep Notes

Leading the D-Team Experience
(60 min. total)

🕐 **(5 min.)**

GET STARTED

Unit Preview
Have a student read aloud the following information from the "Preview" in the Student Notes: *As you work together through "Unit 3: Keep the Faith," you will discover how to walk by faith by answering three questions:*
1. *What is faith?*
2. *Why have faith?*
3. *How do I live by faith?*

Unit Memory Verse
Read aloud James 2:17, "In the same way, faith by itself, if it is not accompanied by action, is dead," and explain that legitimate faith is proved by actions.

Student Prayer
Ask a student to pray that God will show each D-Team member what it means to have faith.

Focus
Share with your D-Team members that during this D-Team experience they will discover what faith is by understanding two essential factors of faith:

Faith Factor #1: Trust
Faith Factor #2: Action

🕐 **(40 min.)**

THE EXPERIENCE

Choose one of the following activities that best fits your D-Team members.

Option A: Trust Fall
Begin your D-Team experience with a "trust fall." Have one student stand on a tall object (table or counter) facing away from the students. Position the rest of the students so that they can catch the student when you give him or her the signal to fall. Then ask the student to fall straight back into the other students' arms. As the student falls, he or she will personally experience what it means to trust and then act on that trust.

Option B: Trust Walk
Pair up your students and give one student in each pair a blindfold to wear throughout the walk. Proceed to take them on a short walk around your building with some difficult maneuvering. Ask partners to switch halfway.

The Equation
After completing either Option A or Option B, ask your D-Team members: **How would you define faith?** Provide your students with some resource materials such as a dictionary or a Bible concordance to assist them in arriving at a definition. Then present the following definition of faith: Trust + Action = Faith.

Faith Factor #1: Trust

Have your students open their Bibles to **Matthew 8:5–13**. Explain that, through this story, they are going to see the essential factors of faith. Ask a student to read the passage. Then share with your students that a centurion was a career military officer in the Roman army who had control over one hundred soldiers. This particular centurion was a Gentile who had not been brought up to know a loving God.

Discuss the following questions. You may want to use the bulleted statements if your students are having a difficult time answering the questions.

Put yourself in the centurion's shoes. What obstacles could have come between Jesus and the centurion, preventing him from trusting Jesus for help?
- The centurion's pride. He probably didn't ask for help very often.
- The centurion's race. He was a Gentile and Jesus was a Jew.
- The centurion's doubt that Jesus could help him with his problem.
- The centurion's fear that Jesus wouldn't accept him.
- The centurion's prestige, money, or power. He could have trusted someone else for help.

Many obstacles could have prevented him from trusting, but the centurion approached Jesus anyway. Look at verses 5–8 and describe the centurion's trust for Jesus.
- He called Him "Lord."
- He believed that Jesus was "big enough" to handle his problem and asked for help.
- He trusted Jesus when Jesus said, "I will go and heal him" (v. 7).

Faith Factor #2: Action

As a result of the centurion's trust, he was able to take action. What were the action steps he took?
- He approached the Lord.
- He asked for help.
- He believed that Jesus could "just say the word" and the centurion's servant would be healed.
- He followed Jesus' command to "Go," and the servant was healed.

What was the result of the centurion's faith in action?
- Jesus praised the man's faith.
- Jesus said the servant would be healed just as the centurion had believed.
- The servant was healed at that hour.

In summary, the centurion trusted that Jesus was Lord. He took a step of action by asking for help and believing in Jesus' promise. The centurion had faith in that promise and, as a result, the servant was healed. The result of Trust + Action = Faith is powerful.

REFLECTION

(5 min.)

Distribute the mustard seeds and clothespins bearing the Bible reference. Remind your students that they just learned that Trust + Action = Faith. Have your students look up Matthew 17:20 and see how Jesus describes the power of faith. Help your students understand the verse by discussing the following questions:
- ***What does God want you to know as you look at the mustard seed?***
- ***As you look at the size of the mustard seed, how much faith do you need? What can you learn from this verse?***
- ***As you are holding the clothespin in your hand, think about your life. Do***

you have any "mountains" that you need to trust Jesus with? Do you have problems that seem too big to handle, or is there something you have not yet trusted Jesus with?
- *Write down your "mountain" and share it with someone in the group.*

As your students share, you may need to remind them that not all their mountains may "move" immediately. God's timing may not always be what we expect, but He is always faithful.

Give your students a few moments to record honest responses to the following questions, found in their Student Notes: **What was most meaningful to you about our experience today? What does God want you to do in response?**

Ask a student to read aloud the Summary Statements in the Student Notes.

Summary Statements

We learned today that . . .
- We can know what faith is by understanding that trust is an essential factor in faith.
- We can know what faith is by understanding that action is the second essential factor in faith.
- Trust plus action equals faith.

🕐 *(10 min.)*

MAKE AN IMPACT

. . . In Your Life
Remind your students that faith means trusting God and then acting on that trust. Challenge your students to choose a "mountain" in their lives that they need to trust God with. Possible mountains might include a difficult test in school, a relationship, a family problem, or a decision about the future.

Ask your students to place their clothespins and mustard seeds in a place where they can see them daily and remember that God is big enough to move mountains.

Then ask them to commit to taking one small step toward trusting God or taking action during this week. For example, a first step toward trusting God with a relational conflict might consist of committing that relationship to prayer and asking Jesus for help.

. . . With Accountability
Have the D-Team members form pairs to become accountability partners for the week and to work on the memory verse. Have each student begin learning the **Unit Memory Verse** by writing it out in the space provided in the Student Notes.

Prayer
Bring the students back together and close in prayer.

1. Faith Equation

Preview

As you work together through "Unit 3: Keep the Faith," you will discover you can walk by faith by answering three questions:

1. What is faith?
2. Why have faith?
3. How do I live by faith?

Unit Memory Verse

"In the same way, faith by itself, if it is not accompanied by action, is dead" (James 2:17).

Focus

This week, you will discover what faith is by understanding two essential factors of faith.

THE EXPERIENCE

The Equation

How would you define faith?

Faith Factor #1: Trust

Read Matthew 8:5–13. Put yourself in the centurion's shoes. What obstacles could have come between Jesus and the centurion, preventing him from trusting Jesus for help?

MAKE AN IMPACT

. . . In Your Life

Faith is trusting God and then acting on that trust. Choose a "mountain" in your life that you need to trust God with. Possible mountains might include a difficult test in school, a relationship, a family problem, or a decision about the future.

Place your clothespin and mustard seed in a place where you can see them daily and remember that God is big enough to move mountains. Then commit to taking one small step toward trusting God or taking action during this week. For example, a first step toward trusting God with a relational conflict might consist of committing that relationship to prayer and asking Jesus for help.

. . . With Accountability

With your accountability partner, talk about your responses to the "Reflection" questions. Exchange phone numbers. Call each other this week to hold each other accountable to making an impact in your life.

name	phone

Begin learning your memory verse by writing it out in the space below.

MEMORY VERSE
James 2:17

Many obstacles could have prevented him from trusting, but the centurion approached Jesus anyway. Look at verses 5–8 and describe the centurion's trust for Jesus.

Faith Factor #2: Action
As a result of the centurion's trust, he was able to take action. What were the action steps he took?

What was the result of the centurion's faith in action?

R E F L E C T I O N

After your leader distributes the mustard seeds and clothespins, take a look at Matthew 17:20 and see how Jesus describes the power of faith.

What does God want you to know as you look at the mustard seed?

As you look at the size of the mustard seed, how much faith do you need?

What can you learn from this verse?

As you are holding the clothespin in your hand, think about your life. Do you have any "mountains" that you need to trust Jesus with? Do you have problems that seem too big to handle, or is there something you have not yet trusted Jesus with?

Write down your "mountain" and share it with someone in the group.

What was most meaningful to you about our experience today?

What does God want you to do in response?

Summary Statements

We learned today that . . .
- We can know what faith is by understanding that trust is an essential factor in faith.
- We can know what faith is by understanding that action is the second essential factor in faith.
- Trust plus action equals faith.

Faith Builders

Before the D-Team Experience

LEADER DEVOTION

If you are good, I'll give you a treat. I promise.
Cross my heart and hope to die. Stick a needle in my eye! I promise.
Of course I don't *like* anybody else! I promise.
For better or for worse, for richer or for poorer, till death do us part. I promise.

Promises. We first hear them when we are young children, but we quickly learn that they are often broken. We learn that there is risk involved in trust. Sadly, those closest to us are often the ones who teach us this difficult lesson. As a result, trust becomes something like a bank account. We keep a "faith account" on everybody. When people break a promise, we make a painful withdrawal from their account. When people keep a promise, a very precious deposit is made.

What does your "faith account" on God look like right now? Are you daily making deposits and remembering the promises He has made for you? Or has your idea of God been twisted somewhere down the line? Maybe you learned at an early age not to trust *anybody*—and now you can't seem to trust even God. Maybe you're dealing with a storm or trial in your life and you have been making mental withdrawals from your account on God, because you don't feel He is carrying through on His promises.

In this D-Team experience, we are going learn that the reason we can have faith in God is that His promises are always trustworthy. Today, ask God to show you a new promise you can hold on to. Make a deposit in your trust account. As you prepare to lead, jot down your personal experiences and insights in the "Prep Notes" column so you can share them with your students.

LOOKING AHEAD

Student Focus
During this D-Team experience, your students will have an opportunity to be assured of God's faithfulness by practicing two faith builders:

Faith Builder #1: Know God's promises.
Faith Builder #2: Remember God's faithfulness.

Unit Memory Verse
"In the same way, faith by itself, if it is not accompanied by action, is dead" (James 2:17).

Practical Impact
During this D-Team experience, you and your students will have the opportunity to remember God's promises in a tangible way—through the building of an altar. This altar will serve as a remembrance that we can trust in God because His promises are true. Choose a place for your altar where you can revisit it as a D-Team and remember God's promises or even add more.

BE PREPARED

Materials Needed
- Bibles and pens
- Duplicated Student Notes
- Checkbook, deposit slip, withdrawal slip (Option 1)
- Rocks (or bricks) and markers (Option A)
- Posterboard and markers (Option B)
- One large rock and markers (Option C)

Special Preparation
- Be ready to explain how to make deposits and withdrawals from a checking account.
- Be prepared to share a personal story of broken and regained trust.

Environment
To set up the environment for this D-Team experience, you can choose one of the following. Option 1 works in any setting; Option 2 moves the experience outside your normal setting.

Option 1: This D-Team experience begins with a discussion about the "faith accounts" we keep on people and God. Bring a checkbook, deposit slip, and withdrawal slip. Be prepared to explain to your students how to make deposits and withdrawals from a checking account.

Option 2: At the beginning of your D-Team experience, take your students to a bank drive-through or ATM. Make a deposit or withdrawal to illustrate the "faith accounts" we keep on other people and God.

Leading the D-Team Experience
(60 min. total)

GET STARTED

Review
Have a student read aloud the information under "Review" in the Student Notes: **Last week you were challenged to take one step toward trusting God or taking an action of faith. What truths did you learn about God? Did you find yourself doing anything differently during the week as a result? In what ways were you encouraged or challenged?**

Student Prayer
Have students form prayers to pray together that the D-Team experience will be a time of growth.

Focus
Share with your students that, during this D-Team experience, they will have an opportunity to be assured of God's faithfulness by practicing two faith builders:

> Faith Builder #1: Know God's promises.
> Faith Builder #2: Remember God's faithfulness.

THE EXPERIENCE

Say: **Think about a person in whom you lost and then gained trust. Describe how you felt when trust was broken. What allowed you to trust again?**

Share your own personal story of broken and regained trust with your D-Team members. Describe how you had a personal "bank account" on this person. When your trust was broken, you took a withdrawal out on your "faith account." As a result, you didn't know if you could really trust this person again. When this person regained your trust, you made a personal deposit in your "faith account." Use a checkbook, deposit slip, and withdrawal slip to make the illustration clearer. Explain that the more deposits made, the more you were able to trust and have faith in this person.

Emphasize that the only person in whom we can have complete faith is God. His promises are never broken. His promises are always true. And yet, obstacles get in the way and we don't always trust Him. Ask your students: **Describe your "faith account" on God.** Then let your students know that they can make a deposit into their "faith account" with God by practicing two faith-builders.

Faith Builder #1: Know God's promises.
The first faith-builder we need to practice is to know God's promises. Have your students take turns looking up the following passages and summarizing the promises God makes in each. Encourage them to circle the promises in their Student Notes that relate to the storms and trials in their lives.

> **Psalm 30:5** (promise of God's favor)
> **Psalm 34:19** (promise of deliverance)
> **Isaiah 43:2** (promise of God's presence in troubled times)
> **Mark 11:24** (promise of answered prayer)

John 6:35 (promise of spiritual fullness)
John 12:46 (promise of spiritual light)
John 14:1–2 (promise of an eternal home)
John 14:12 (promise of spiritual power)
Romans 4:21 (promise that God's promises are true)
Romans 8:28; 2 Corinthians 4:17 (promise that all things work for the believer's good)
2 Corinthians 12:9 (promise of sufficient grace and power in weakness)
1 John 2:25 (promise of eternal life)
Revelation 21:4 (promise of future deliverance from sorrow and pain)

After reading God's promises, ask volunteers to share the promises that relate to their lives. Encourage each student to personalize those promises by rewriting the promises with his or her name in them.

Faith Builder #2: Remember God's faithfulness.
The second faith-builder is remembering God's faithfulness in carrying out what He promised. Share with your students how people of faith in the Old Testament often built altars in response to experiencing God's faithfulness in their lives. These altars were reminders of God's promises and were faith-builders for people when they encountered storms in life and had difficulty trusting God's plan. In your own words, share God's promise and Abraham's response in Genesis 17:1–7.

Then ask your students to think quietly about a time when they experienced God's faithfulness to a promise. You may even want to ask your students to take a few minutes and find a quiet place to think about this time in their lives.

 (5 min.)

REFLECTION

After your students have taken time to remember God's faithfulness in their lives, explain to your students that they are going to have the opportunity to remember God's promises in a tangible way—by building an altar. This altar will serve as a remembrance that we can trust God because His promises are true. Choose one of the following ways for your D-Team to build an altar:

Option A
Provide your D-Team members with rocks or bricks and have each person write something on a rock that represents a promise to which God has been faithful in their lives. Then stack the rocks in an area where they will be undisturbed—on your lawn, in a corner of the church parking lot, in a park, or even in a member's basement. As each person places a rock on the altar, ask that person to share his or her story.

Option B
Have your D-Team members make a banner or posters of God's promises that they have experienced as true in their lives.

Option C
Have your D-Team members locate a very large rock and write God's faithful promises on the rock.

Whatever you decide to do, try to choose a place for your altar that your students can revisit to recall God's promises or even add more promises.

After building your altar, praise God for being the One in whom we can have faith.

Give your students a few moments to record honest responses to the following questions, found in their Student Notes: **What was most meaningful to you about our experience today? What does God want you to do in response?**

Ask a student to read aloud the Summary Statements in the Student Notes.

Summary Statements

We learned today that . . .
- God has given us many promises.
- God is always faithful in doing what He has promised.
- We can have faith in God because His promises are always true.
- We can be assured of God's faithfulness by knowing God's promises and remembering His faithfulness in the past.

MAKE AN IMPACT

(10 min.)

. . . In Your Life
Challenge each student to make a personal plan to practice one of the faith builders during the week. Suggest the following plans:

Plan #1: Claim one of God's promises as their own and memorize it.
Plan #2: Read one promise of God each day.
Plan #3: Return to the altar during the week and quietly meditate on God's faithfulness.
Plan #4: Build a personal altar.
Plan #5: Each morning, ask God to show them His faithfulness and every evening write down what they learned.

. . . With Accountability
Have the D-Team members form pairs to become accountability partners for the week and to work on the memory verse. Have each student write out the **Unit Memory Verse** and recite it to his or her partner.

Prayer
Bring your students together and close in prayer.

2. Faith Builders

Review

Last week you were challenged to take one step toward trusting God or taking an action of faith. What truths did you learn about God?

Did you find yourself doing anything differently during the week as a result?

In what ways were you encouraged or challenged?

Focus

This week, you will have an opportunity to be assured of God's faithfulness by practicing two faith builders.

THE EXPERIENCE

Think about a person in whom you lost and then gained trust. Describe how you felt when trust was broken. What allowed you to trust again?

Describe your "faith account" on God.

Plan #4: Build a personal altar.

Plan #5: Each morning, ask God to show you His faithfulness and every evening write down what you learned.

. . . With Accountability

With your accountability partner, talk about your responses to the "Reflection" questions. Exchange phone numbers. Call each other this week to hold each other accountable to making an impact in your life.

name _____ phone _____

Review your memory verse by writing it out in the space below. Then recite it to your partner.

M E M O R Y   V E R S E
James 2:17

Faith Builder #1: Know God's promises.

Check out the following promises of God. Circle the promises that relate to the storms and trials in your life.

Psalm 30:5

Psalm 34:19

Isaiah 43:2

Mark 11:24

John 6:35

John 12:46

John 14:1–2

John 14:12

Romans 4:21

Romans 8:28; 2 Corinthians 4:17

2 Corinthians 12:9

1 John 2:25

Revelation 21:4

Be prepared to share the promises that relate to your life. Personalize the promise that relates to you by rewriting the promise with your name in it.

Faith Builder #2: Remember God's faithfulness.
Think about a time when you experienced God's faithfulness to a promise.

REFLECTION

What was most meaningful to you about our experience today?

What does God want you to do in response?

Summary Statements

We learned today that . . . .
- God has given us many promises.
- God is always faithful in doing what He has promised.
- We can have faith in God because His promises are always true.
- We can be assured of God's faithfulness by knowing God's promises and remembering His faithfulness in the past.

MAKE AN IMPACT

. . . In Your Life
Choose one of the following personal plans to practice one of the faith builders during the week:

Plan #1: Claim one of God's promises as your own and memorize it.
Plan #2: Read one promise of God each day.
Plan #3: Return to the altar during the week and quietly meditate on God's faithfulness.

Faith in Action

Before the D-Team Experience

LEADER DEVOTION

"'Lord, if it's You,' Peter replied, 'tell me to come to you on the water.' 'Come,' he said. Then Peter got down out of the boat, walked on the water and came toward Jesus. But when he saw the wind, he was afraid and, beginning to sink, cried out, 'Lord, save me!' Immediately Jesus reached out his hand and caught him. 'You of little faith,' he said, 'why did you doubt?'" (Matt. 14:28–31).

Peter knew what faith was and that he could trust Jesus. Yet something went wrong. What happened? When Peter saw the wind, he *took his eyes off Jesus.* He felt the fear and *took his eyes off Jesus.* He began to doubt and *took his eyes off Jesus.*

So many times we begin to put our faith into action and find ourselves sinking, because we took our eyes off Jesus. Our fears and doubts overwhelm us. They become stumbling blocks that prevent us from experiencing the power of faith. When was the last time you found yourself in Peter's shoes? What prevented you from taking the steps Jesus was asking you to take? Have you had the opportunity to share Christ with a family member or co-worker and found yourself not taking that step because you fear what they will think or that you won't know what to say? Are you in an unhealthy dating relationship you need to terminate, but haven't, because you fear losing love and doubt that Christ can fill that need? Do you need to confront somebody in love, but are avoiding the conflict because of overwhelming fear and doubt? What fears and doubts are immobilizing you?

Write those fears down, study the following D-Team experience, and commit to taking the same steps you are asking your students to take. As you prepare to lead, jot down your personal experiences and insights in the "Prep Notes" column so you can share them with your students.

LOOKING AHEAD

During this D-Team experience, your students will discover how to walk by faith by taking two action steps:

    Action Step #1: Stand up.
    Action Step #2: Look to Jesus.

Unit Memory Verse
"In the same way, faith by itself, if it is not accompanied by action, is dead" (James 2:17).

Practical Impact
After your students have studied the story of Peter walking on water, they will experience the first steps of walking by faith. They will be given the opportunity to approach the altar they made last week and prayerfully offer the doubts and fears that prevent them from taking the steps of faith God is asking them to take. This will be a powerful time of commitment and faith for you and your students.

BE PREPARED

Materials Needed
- Bibles and pens
- Duplicated Student Sheets
- A notecard for each student
- A video clip, stuffed animal, storybook, etc. (Option 1)

Environment
To set up the environment for this D-Team experience, you can choose one of the following. Option 1 works in any setting; Option 2 moves the experience outside your normal setting.

Option 1: Bring a video clip, stuffed animal, storybook, etc., that represents a fear you had as a child.

Option 2: Have your students return to the altar they made last week. Be sure that there are few distractions so that your students can be transparent and open with each other.

Leading the D-Team Experience
(60 min. total)

GET STARTED

Review
Have a student read aloud the information under "Review" in the Student Notes: *Last week you were challenged to practice a faith-builder during the week. What truths did you learn about God? Did you find yourself doing anything differently during the week? In what ways were you encouraged or challenged?*

Focus
Share with your students that this week they will discover how to walk with faith by taking two action steps:

Action Step #1: Stand up.
Action Step #2: Look to Jesus.

THE EXPERIENCE

Action Step #1: Stand up.
Ask: *What were you afraid of when you were a child?* The purpose of this time will be to help your students become more comfortable about being transparent about their current fears.

Share your own personal story of fear and how you needed to stand up against it. Then explain that, as we grow older, some fears, like the monster under the bed, disappear, but other fears get bigger and become more real. Fear and doubt can become so real that they immobilize us. It can seem almost impossible to stand up against our fears and doubts.

Have a student **read aloud Matthew 14:22–32,** a story about someone who needed to confront his doubts and fears and "stand up."

Share that Peter took his first step toward walking with faith—he stood up against fear and doubt even when the other disciples were afraid. But Peter did not stand up for long. In fact, he started to sink!

Have your students **look at verses 29–30 again.** Ask: *What prevented Peter from walking with faith?* (He was afraid of the wind; he started to doubt that he could walk on water; he took his eyes off Jesus and began to sink as a result of doubt and fear.)

Action Step #2: Look to Jesus.
Bottom line, Peter took his eyes off Jesus. He forgot who Jesus was and became focused on his doubt and fears. Instruct your students: *Read the following verses and write down what the disciples already knew about Jesus.*

Matthew 6:25–27—Jesus taught His disciples not to worry about their lives; that just as God provides for the birds, He will also provide for you. He also taught them that worrying is more harmful than helpful.

Prep Notes

Matthew 8:23–27—Jesus showed His disciples that when we follow Jesus, there is no need to fear. When you need help from Jesus, just ask; Jesus is bigger than any problem. Even the winds and waves obey Him!

Matthew 14:22–32—Jesus told His disciples: "Get into the boat and go ahead of Me" and "Take courage! It is I. Don't be afraid" and "Come."

Summarize that when we look to Jesus, we remember the truths that we've been learning in this unit and can walk through our fears and doubts. Ask your students to share some truths from their previous D-Team experiences that will help them stand up and look to Jesus. Add the following to your students' list: **Trust + Action = Faith that can move mountains.** God's promises are true. God is always faithful to His promises.

⏱ *(5 min.)*

REFLECTION

Share that walking with faith is a lot like walking a tightrope. When you look down, your fears can overcome you and you begin to wobble. In the same way, if we focus on the wind and waves of storms in our lives instead of Jesus, we will begin to sink. Romans 8:15 tells us, "For you did not receive a spirit that makes you a slave again to fear." In other words, as a Christian, you are no longer slaves to sin, but free in Christ.

Read Psalm 27 aloud in unison to discover what happens when we stand up, look to Jesus, and overcome fear and doubt.

Distribute the notecards to your D-Team members. Tell your students that they do not have to be controlled by fear and doubt. Ask them to think about a step of faith that Jesus is asking them to take. Offer the following examples of steps: witness to a friend, deal with a conflict, apply to a college, or trust Jesus with a family problem. Then, have them write on their notecards a fear or doubt that has been preventing them from taking that step of faith. They'll use these notecards at the end of your time together.

Give your students a few moments to record honest responses to the following questions, found in their Student Notes: **What was most meaningful to you about our experience today? What does God want you to do in response?**

Ask a student to read aloud the Summary Statements in the Student Notes.

Summary Statements

We learned today that . . .
- We can walk with faith by taking the two action steps of standing up and looking to Jesus.
- When we look to Jesus, we remember the truths we've learned and can walk through our fears and doubts.

MAKE AN IMPACT

. . . In Your Life

Take your students to the altar you built during the last D-Team experience. Ask your students to take the step of walking in faith by prayerfully taking their notecards with the fears or doubts written on them and placing them on the altar. In doing this, your students will be committing to stand up and look to Jesus. Another option would be to have your D-Team members destroy their notecards as a symbol of overcoming their fears. As D-Team members place their notecards on the altar, have them share the steps they are going to take.

. . . With Accountability

Have the D-Team members form pairs to become accountability partners for the week and to work on the memory verse. Have each student write out the **Unit Memory Verse**, recite it to his or her partner, and share a way the verse is meaningful in his or her life.

Prayer

Bring the students back together and close in prayer.

3. Faith in Action

Review your memory verse by writing it out in the space below. After reciting it to your partner, share a way the verse is meaningful in your life.

MEMORY VERSE
James 2:17

Review
Last week, you were challenged to practice a faith-builder during the week. What truths did you learn about God?

Did you find yourself doing anything differently during the week?

In what ways were you encouraged or challenged?

Focus
During this experience, you will discover how to walk in faith by taking two action steps.

THE EXPERIENCE

Action Step #1: Stand up.
What were you afraid of when you were a child?

Read Matthew 14:22–32. Look at verses 29–30 again. What prevented Peter from walking in faith?

Action Step #2: Look to Jesus.

Read the following verses and write down what the disciples already knew about Jesus.

Matthew 6:25-27—Jesus taught His disciples . . . .

Matthew 8:23-27—Jesus showed His disciples . . . .

Matthew 14:22-32—Jesus told His disciples . . . .

REFLECTION

Read Psalm 27. What happens when we stand up, look to Jesus, and overcome fear and doubt?

We do not have to be controlled by fear and doubt. What is a step of faith Jesus is asking you to take?

Write down the fear or doubt that is preventing you from taking that step of faith.

What was most meaningful to you about our experience today?

What does God want you to do in response?

Summary Statements

We learned today that . . . .
- We can walk with faith by taking the two action steps of standing up and looking to Jesus.
- When we look to Jesus, we remember the truths that we've learned and can walk through our fears and doubts.

MAKE AN IMPACT

. . . In Your Life

Visit the altar you built last week. Take the step of walking in faith by prayerfully taking your notecard with the fear or doubt written on it and placing it on the altar. In doing this, you are committing to stand up and look to Jesus. As you place your card on the altar, be prepared to share the step you are going to take.

. . . With Accountability

With your accountability partner, talk about your responses to the "Reflection" questions. Exchange phone numbers. Call each other this week to hold each other accountable to making an impact in your life.

OBEDIENCE

LEADER FOCUS

To be like Christ.
That is our goal, plain and simple. It sounds like a peaceful, relaxing, easy objective.
But stop and think.
He learned obedience by the things he suffered.
So must we.
It is neither easy nor quick nor natural.
It is ipossible in the flesh, slow in coming, and suprenatural in scope.
Only Christ can accomplish it within us.

Chuck Swindoll,
as quoted in *Draper's Book of Christian Quotations* (Wheaton, IL: Tyndale, 1992)

You can take your students through this unit, but unless *Christ* changes their hearts, it is all in vain. Spend time right now praying for Christ's work in your students' hearts.

BIG PICTURE

Unit Overview
In Unit 4 we will be focusing on living an obedient life to God by answering three questions: (1) What is obedience? (2) How does God tell us what we should obey? (3) How does God want us to be obedient?

1. Free at Last
During this D-Team experience, your students will discover what obedience is by recognizing two perceptions of obedience:

Perception #1: Obedience is restrictive and controlling.
Perception #2: Obedience is the key to freedom.

2. Voice Lessons
During this D-Team experience, your students will discover how to identify God's voice by accessing four important tools:

Tool #1: God's Word
Tool #2: Prayer
Tool #3: Other Christians
Tool #4: Our Circumstances

3. Turning Points
During this D-Team experience, your students will discover how to be obedient by taking three turning points:

Turning Point #1: Determine what area in life God is asking us to obey Him.
Turning Point #2: Determine what action should be taken.
Turning Point #3: Determine who we want to have in control of our lives.

Unit Memory Verse
"If you love Me, you will obey what I command" (John 14:15).

The Map

Before the D-Team Experience

LEADER DEVOTION

What does obedience mean to you? Are you free or bound by the command to obey God?

> Obedience to Jesus Christ is essential, but not compulsory; he never insists on being Master. We feel that if only he would insist, we should obey him. But our Lord never enforces his "thou shalts" and "thou shalt nots;" he never takes means to force us to do what he says. . . . The term *obey* would be better expressed by the word *use*. For instance, a scientist uses the laws of nature; that is, he more than obeys them, he causes them to fulfill their destiny in his work. That is exactly what happens in the saint's life. He uses the commands of the Lord, and they fulfill God's destiny in his life.
>
> Oswald Chambers, as quoted in *Draper's Book of Quotations,* (Wheaton, IL: Tyndale, 1992), 446.

Take time to evaluate your own obedience before you teach your students. Use this week's study as a devotional. As you prepare for this D-Team experience, jot down your personal experiences and insights in the "Prep Notes" column so you can share them with the students.

LOOKING AHEAD

Student Focus
After this D-Team experience, your students will discover what obedience is by recognizing two perceptions of obedience:

Perception #1: Obedience is restrictive and controlling.
Perception #2: Obedience is the key to freedom.

Unit Memory Verse
"If you love Me, you will obey what I command" (John 14:15).

Practical Impact
During this D-Team experience, you will use a map to illustrate how obeying God's Word helps get you where God's plan is taking you.

BE PREPARED

Materials Needed
- Bibles and pens
- Duplicated Student Sheets
- A local map for each student

Environment

To set up the environment for this D-Team experience, you can choose one of the following. Option 1 works in any setting; Option 2 moves the experience outside your normal setting.

Option 1: Bring several maps to this D-Team experience. Encourage your students to look at them and locate each other's homes. Ask them to pick a destination and determine at least two routes to get from their homes to the destination.

Option 2: Drive your students to a place with which they aren't familiar. Then stop and pull out a map. Ask them to locate where you are. Ask them if there was a better way to get there and which other way you could have gone. Then have your D-Team meet at a park, in a parking lot, or in your car!

Leading the D-Team Experience
(60 min. total)

GET STARTED

Unit Preview
Have a student read aloud the information under the "Preview" in the Student Notes:
As you work together through "Unit 4: Obedience," you will discover how to live an obedient life to God by answering three questions:
1. *What is obedience?*
2. *How does God tell us what we should obey?*
3. *How does God want us to be obedient?*

Unit Memory Verse
Read aloud John 14:15, "If you love Me, you will obey what I command." Emphasize to your students that love, like faith, can't be separated from obedience.

Student Prayer
Ask a D-Team member to pray that God would reveal the positive side of being obedient.

Focus
Share with your D-Team members that this week they will discover what obedience is by recognizing two perceptions of obedience:

Perception #1: Obedience is restrictive and controlling.
Perception #2: Obedience is the key to freedom.

THE EXPERIENCE

Begin this D-Team experience by asking your students: *Do you consider yourself a good "map person"? Why or why not?*

Place a copy of your local map on a table. Ask students to identify all the different reasons you would need a map. Point out that we can look at a map from two perspectives. First, we can view the roads as restricting us to only the places to which they lead. For example, "Why don't they make a road that will take me . . . here!" Or we can view a map as a symbol of freedom: "Look at all the places I can go and the different ways I can get there!"

Ask your students: *What did God really mean when He asked us to be obedient? What words or thoughts come to mind when you hear the word obey?* Their answers may include rules, boundaries, rebellion, submission, being controlled by someone else, doing what someone asks or tells you to do, etc.

Point out that *Webster's* states the definition to be: "To hear, to carry out the instructions or orders of; to be guided by; submit to the control of." Ask: *Which of these sounds more appealing: to be "guided by" or "controlled by" someone else? Why?*

Perception #1: Obedience is restrictive and controlling.
Perception #2: Obedience is the key to freedom.

Prep Notes

(These perceptions will be dealt with concurrently throughout the D-Team experience.)

Remember how we said that we could look at the local map in two different ways? That's how obedience works. We can look at it as restrictive and controlling, or we can see it as freedom! Let's take out another map, the one that God gave us to use and obey: the Word of God.

There are things on this "map" that could be looked at in those two ways also. We can go to any of the places on God's map, and there are many ways to get there. We just have to stay on the roads that will get us there. We just need to be obedient. God's Word could be a book of rules that restricts where we go, what we do, or how we get there.

Or there is the way that God intended—a book of freedom. The guidelines are for our protection. Disobedience would be like trying to travel across the country without a map. No directions. Where will we most likely end up? Not where we wanted to go, and maybe even into a dangerous place or situation.

Ask: ***Have you ever gotten lost trying to follow directions someone gave you? How did it make you feel? Mad? Frustrated? Confused? Lost? Angry at the person that gave you the directions, or at yourself?***

Explain that there are usually two reasons why we get lost. Either we didn't check an official map to see if the directions we were given would take us to our destination or we thought we knew a quicker or better way—a short cut. So we turned off the road on which we were supposed to stay.

Both of these situations can be applied to obeying the Word of God. There are times when the advice of someone takes us a direction that we didn't want to go, because we didn't check its validity against God's Word. There are also times where we think we know a quicker or easier or better way to do something instead of obeying the way God told us. God calls that disobedience—not trusting His judgment.

Have your students take a look at some verses that will give them God's perspective on obedience. Give each of your students a Scripture passage and have them share with the others what they learned about obedience.

Psalm 25:8–10 (God will teach us how to be obedient. He won't leave us guessing.)
Proverbs 10:29 (The way of the Lord is a refuge.)
Isaiah 1:19–20 (Gives the benefits of obedience and the downfalls of disobedience.)
Matthew 7:24–25 (Not only hearing, but putting God's ways into practice.)
Luke 11:28 (Blessed are those who obey.)
John 15:10–11 (If we obey, we will remain in His love and will have true joy.)
Romans 2:13 (Those who not only hear but obey will be declared righteous.)
1 John 1:3–6 (Obeying is a natural response to knowing God. The more we know about Him, the more we will want to obey Him.)

God made a map by which we can live if we follow it by obeying its commands. Don't you think He knows the best way to travel? He can help us map out the best plans for our lives. But each of us has to consciously make the decision daily to stay on the best road that will get us there. He promised us many things in the verses we looked up earlier. If we decide to believe that God has a plan for our life and we want to do it the best way possible, then we are saying we want to be obedient.

REFLECTIONS

Today, your students learned two different ways to look at obedience to God: as restrictive or freeing. Ask: *Will you make the choice today to do things God's way? To follow His directions? Or are you going to do things your own way?*

Give your students a few moments to record honest responses to the following questions, found in their Student Notes: *What was most meaningful to you about our experience today? What does God want you to do in response?*

Ask a student to read aloud the Summary Statements in the Student Notes.

Summary Statements

We learned today that . . .
- God commands us to be obedient.
- God intended obedience to be a pathway to freedom, not restrictions.
- Obedience will take us exactly where God intends us to be.

MAKE AN IMPACT

. . . In Your Life
Tell your students that if they made the decision to go God's direction, then the next step would be to get up every morning this next week and consciously make the choice to obey God.

Ask your D-Team members to take five minutes to tell God that they want to obey Him and to ask Him to help them. Distribute copies of the local map and suggest they put it in their Bibles to remind them of God's directions, which provide the *best* possible route for their lives. Be sure to ask your students to bring their maps to the next D-Team gathering.

. . . With Accountability
Have the D-Team members form pairs to become accountability partners for the week and to work on the memory verse. Have each student begin learning the **Unit Memory Verse** by writing it out in the space provided in the Student Notes.

Prayer
Bring the students back together and close in prayer.

4. The Map

Preview

As you work together through "Unit 4: Obedience," you will discover how to live an obedient life to God by answering three questions:

1. What is obedience?
2. How does God tell us what we should obey?
3. How does God want us to be obedient?

Unit Memory Verse

"If you love Me, you will obey what I command" (John 14:15).

Focus

This week, you will discover what obedience is by recognizing two perceptions of obedience.

THE EXPERIENCE

Do you consider yourself a good "map person"? Why or why not?

What did God really mean when He asked us to be obedient? What words or thoughts come to mind when you hear the word obey?

Which of these sounds more appealing: to be "guided by" or "controlled by" someone else? Why?

MAKE AN IMPACT

. . . In Your Life

If you made the decision to go God's direction, then the next step would be to get up every morning this next week and consciously make the choice to obey God.

Take five minutes to tell God that you want to obey Him and to ask Him to help you. Put your copy of the map in your Bible to remind you of God's directions, which provide the best possible route for your life. Be sure to bring your map next week.

. . . With Accountability

With your accountability partner, talk about your responses to the "Reflection" questions. Exchange phone numbers. Call each other this week to hold each other accountable to making an impact in your life.

name _____ phone _____

Begin learning your memory verse by writing it out in the space below.

MEMORY VERSE
John 14:15

Perception #1: Obedience is restrictive and controlling.

Perception #2: Obedience is the key to freedom.

Have you ever gotten lost trying to follow directions someone gave you?

How did it make you feel? Mad? Frustrated? Confused? Lost? Angry at the person that gave you the directions, or at yourself?

Take a look at some verses that will give you God's perspective on obedience. Then be prepared to share what you learned about obedience.

Psalm 25:8–10—

Proverbs 10:29—

Isaiah 1:19–20—

Matthew 7:24–25—

Luke 11:28—

John 15:10–11—

Romans 2:13—

1 John 1:3–6—

REFLECTIONS

Today, you learned two different ways to look at obedience to God: as restrictive or freeing. Will you make the choice today to do things God's way? To follow His directions? Or are you going to do things your own way?

What was most meaningful to you about our experience today?

What does God want you to do in response?

Summary Statements

We learned today that . . .

- God commands us to be obedient.
- God intended obedience to be a pathway to freedom, not restrictions.
- Obedience will take us exactly where God intends us to be.

Voice Lessons

Before the D-Team Experience

LEADER DEVOTION

When was the last time you heard God's voice? Shhh. Be silent for a moment. Close your eyes and see how long you can be quiet. Don't fall asleep! You have to be quiet to hear God's voice. Take some time to tune into God's voice. Don't pass up the opportunity to hear what He is trying to tell you. Your students need to know that God speaks today and that He can work in their lives. Be prepared to share with your students a fresh new experience with God. Jot down your personal experiences and insights in the "Prep Notes" column so you can share them with the students.

LOOKING AHEAD

Student Focus
During this D-Team experience, your students will discover how to identify God's voice by accessing four important tools:

Tool #1: God's Word
Tool #2: Prayer
Tool #3: Other Christians
Tool #4: Our circumstances

Unit Memory Verse
"If you love Me, you will obey what I command" (John 14:15).

Practical Impact
During this D-Team experience, you will illustrate to your students the different tools they need in order to use the map properly. Your students will learn about four tools that will help them read a different map God has drawn for us.

BE PREPARED

Materials Needed
- Bibles and pens
- Duplicated Student Sheets
- A local map
- Maps, compasses, etc. (Option 1)

Special Preparation
Contact your D-Team members and remind them to bring the maps they received last week to this week's gathering.

Environment

To set up the environment for this D-Team experience, you can choose one of the following. Option 1 works in any setting; Option 2 moves the experience outside your normal setting.

Option 1: Bring maps, compasses, and any other tools that can be used to read a map. As your students arrive, encourage them to examine and try out these tools.

Option 2: Take your D-Team members on another mystery ride (see Option 2 from last week). Tell them to watch carefully where you are going. When you get there, pull out the map again and ask them to locate where they are. Again, you can have your study right there or go back to a house or the church.

Leading the D-Team Experience
(60 min. total)

GET STARTED

(5 min.) 🕐

Review

Have a student read aloud the information under "Review" in the Student Notes: *Last week, you learned about two different perceptions of obedience. You were challenged to make a choice daily to obey God. If you took the next step by praying five minutes a day and asking Him to help you obey Him, then share with the other students how it made a difference in your life.*

Focus

Share with your D-Team members that during this D-Team experience they will discover how to identify God's voice by accessing four important tools:

> **Tool #1: God's Word**
> **Tool #2: Prayer**
> **Tool #3: Other Christians**
> **Tool #4: Our circumstances**

THE EXPERIENCE

(40 min.) 🕐

Place a local map on a table. (If your students remembered to bring their maps this week, have them look on their own copies.) Ask: *Identify some of the different features on the map that need to be there so that it can be used properly.*

Share the following with your students: *Here are some of the basic tools we will talk about today:*

A Compass
A compass tells us which way would be north on the map. North will always be the same direction. South will always point the opposite of north. East and west will always oppose each other. We can count on it.

Roads and Highways
Roads and highways give us options. Without them, it would be impossible to figure out how to get from one place to another. Try to imagine a map without the roads shown on it. It would be a bunch of towns and cities and water. Not very helpful!

The Names of Roads, Towns, and Cities
Names distinguish roads, towns, and cities from each other. Try to imagine the map without words—it would be just a ton of lines! How confusing! We would be driving around forever!

The Mileage Gauge
This tells us how long it will take us to get to a destination... Usually one inch equals a certain amount of miles.

Spiritual Tools
Explain that obeying God depends on a number of things also. Last week, you

decided whether you wanted to do things God's way or your own way. If you believe God wants to accomplish great things through you, then you have to trust Him. You have to obey what direction He wants you to go.

But how do you know what direction that is? *Listening for God's voice is like getting directions from someone. There are four basic tools you can use to help you distinguish His voice.*

Tool #1: God's Word
Have a student *read aloud Proverbs 2:1–2.* Ask: *What do these verses tell us about distinguishing God's voice?* (They tell us that reading God's Word brings us wisdom. God's Word, like a compass, never changes. It's truth in which we can put our trust.)

Tool #2: Prayer
Have a student *read aloud Proverbs 2:3–5.* Ask: *What do these verses tell us about distinguishing God's voice?* (They tell us that spending time in prayer daily connects us to our Heavenly Father.)

Tool #3: Other Christians
Have a student *read aloud Ephesians 4:15–16.* Ask: *What do these verses tell us about distinguishing God's voice?* (They tell us that maturity is possible as we are built up by other members of Christ's body. Christian friends, like the roads on the map, will help us sort out our options.)

Tool #4: Our circumstances
Say: *This is the last tool, because without the other three tools, this one is invalid and unusable. It must agree with what the other three tools tell us.*

We can't just rely on past experiences or other people's stories. When we listen for God's voice, we must make sure that prayer, Scripture, other Christians, and the situation all point in the same direction we think God is asking us to obey Him.

Share with your students that throughout the Bible, when God decided to talk to someone, that person knew what was said and who was talking. The person heard God's voice and was obedient to whatever God told him or her to do. (If you want to go deeper—read about David, Paul, Moses, and Daniel!)
Ask: *Have you ever been in a situation where you "heard God's voice" telling you to say or do something in order to be obedient, but you put it off because it didn't fit into your schedule?*

Remind your students that God doesn't drop suggestions in a box for us to sort through and decide which ones should be done. God is carrying out His will. He wants us to be a part of it by obeying His commands. Let's not miss the opportunity to be obedient by neglecting to use the four tools daily.

 (5 min.)

REFLECTION

Tell your students that today they learned about four tools they can use to help them hear God's voice and determine in what area of their life God is asking them to be obedient. The next step is to actually use these tools. Ask them to identify a tool they have not used very often or not at all, and to try to use it daily for the next week to help them hear God's voice.

Give your students a few moments to record honest responses to the following questions, found in their Student Notes: **What was most meaningful to you about our experience today? What does God want you to do in response?**

Ask a student to read aloud the Summary Statements in the Student Notes.

Summary Statements

We learned today that . . .
- God tells us how to obey Him.
- We can hear God's voice through God's Word, prayer, other Christians, and our circumstances.
- The different ways of hearing God's voice should always agree with each other.

MAKE AN IMPACT

(10 min.)

Ask your students to take time this week to determine in what area of their lives God is asking them to be obedient. Ask them to commit to spending ten minutes a day using one or all of the tools that they learned about today. They can pray about it, read God's Word, or talk to other Christians. Then they can assess the situation around them. Suggest that they write down an area in which they need to be obedient, and to bring it to the next D-Team gathering.

. . . With Accountability
Have the D-Team members form pairs to become accountability partners for the week and to work on the memory verse. Have each student write out the **Unit Memory Verse** and recite it to his or her partner.

Prayer
Bring the students back together and close in prayer.

2. Voice Lessons

Review
Last week, you learned about two different perceptions of obedience. You were challenged to make a choice daily to obey God. If you took the next step by praying five minutes a day and asking Him to help you obey Him, then share with the other students how it made a difference in your life.

Focus
This week, you will discover how to identify God's voice by accessing four important tools.

THE EXPERIENCE

Identify some of the features on a map that *need* to be there so that it can be used properly.

Here are some of the basic tools we will talk about today:

A Compass
A compass tells us which way would be north on the map. North will always be the same direction. South will always point the opposite of north. East and west will always oppose each other. We can count on it.

Roads and Highways
Roads and highways give us options. Without them, it would be impossible to figure out how to get from one place to another. Try to imagine a map without the roads shown on it. It would be a bunch of towns and cities and water. Not very helpful!

The Names of Roads, Towns, and Cities
Names distinguish roads, towns, and cities from each other. Try to imagine the map without words—it would be just a ton of lines! How confusing! We would be driving around forever!

MAKE AN IMPACT

... In Your Life
Take time this week to determine in what area of your life God is asking you to be obedient. Commit to spending ten minutes a day using one or all of the tools you learned about today. Pray about it, read God's Word, or talk to other Christians. Then assess your circumstances. Write down an area in which you need to be obedient, and bring it in next week.

... With Accountability
With your accountability partner, talk about your responses to the "Reflection" questions. Exchange phone numbers. Call each other this week to hold each other accountable to making an impact in your life.

name _____ phone _____

Review your memory verse by writing it out in the space below. Then recite it to your partner.

MEMORY VERSE
John 14:15

The Mileage Gauge

This tells us how long it will take us to get to a destination. Usually one inch equals a certain number of miles.

Spiritual Tools

Listening for God's voice is like getting directions from someone. There are four basic tools you can use to help you distinguish His voice.

Tool #1: God's Word

Read Proverbs 2:1-2. What do these verses tell us about distinguishing God's voice?

Tool #2: Prayer

Read Proverbs 2:3-5. What do these verses tell us about distinguishing God's voice?

Tool #3: Other Christians

Read Ephesians 4:15-16. What do these verses tell us about distinguishing God's voice?

Tool #4: Our circumstances

This is the last tool, because without the other three tools, this one is invalid and unusable. It must agree with what the other three tools tell us.

Have you ever been in a situation where you "heard God's voice" telling you to say or do something in order to be obedient, but you put it off because it didn't fit into your schedule?

REFLECTION

Today, you learned about four tools you can use to help you hear God's voice and determine in what area of your life God is asking you to be obedient. The next step is to actually use these tools. Identify a tool you have not used very often or not at all. Try to use it daily for the next week to help you hear God's voice.

What was most meaningful to you about our experience today?

What does God want you to do in response?

Summary Statements

We learned today that . . .
- God tells us how to obey Him.
- We can hear God's voice through God's Word, prayer, other Christians, and our circumstances.
- The different ways of hearing God's voice should always agree with each other.

Turning Points

Before the D-Team Experience

LEADER DEVOTION

Obedience will always be a struggle because we are all sinners. It goes against our human nature to submit to someone else and let him lead us.

When was the last time you knew the right thing to do, yet resisted it for as long as possible before obeying? Or maybe you decided to be disobedient, and did it your own way?

If you can be honest with yourself and admit you are not exempt from this obedience concept you are about to teach, you have just taken the first step to preparing this material. Your students need to know you struggle with obedience too. Take time to be quiet and evaluate your own life for a few minutes.

Is there an area of your life in which God is asking you to be obedient? Are you willing to obey His commands? If you need to take some kind of action out of obedience, then do so before moving on to the study. Jot down your personal experiences and insights in the "Prep Notes" column so you can share them with the students.

LOOKING AHEAD

Student Focus
During this D-Team experience, your students will discover how to be obedient by taking three turning points:

Turning Point #1: Determine what area in life God is asking us to obey Him.
Turning Point #2: Determine what action should be taken.
Turning Point #3: Determine who we want to have in control of our lives.

Unit Memory Verse
"If you love Me, you will obey what I command" (John 14:15).

Practical Impact
During this D-Team experience, you will once again use a map to illustrate the different roads we can take and which are the best possible routes. You will give your students a blank car key to remind them of who is "driving the car" in their lives.

BE PREPARED

Materials Needed
- Bibles and pens
- Duplicated Student Sheets
- A local map
- A blank car key for each student

Special Preparation

Contact your D-Team members and remind them to bring the maps they received two weeks ago to this week's D-Team experience.

Environment

To set up the environment for this D-Team experience, you can choose one of the following. Option 1 works in any setting; Option 2 moves the experience outside your normal setting.

Option 1: Have your students meet somewhere in your church where they can see a road from where they are sitting.

Option 2: Have your D-Team meet right next to the road. If the noise level of traffic is going to be distracting, then meet in a car or van that is parked facing the road.

Leading the D-Team Experience
(60 min. total)

GET STARTED

Review
Have a student read aloud the information under "Review" in the Student Notes: **How does God talk to us? If God wants us to obey Him, how do we know what that means for us?**

Last week, you learned about the different tools on a map that help us read it more effectively. We also learned about the different tools God gave us to understand His "directions."

After completing last week's D-Team experience, your students should be able to tell you the four tools for hearing God's voice: God's Word, prayer, other Christians, and our circumstances. Ask volunteers to share the area of their lives in which God is asking them to obey Him.

Focus
Share with your D-Team members that they will discover how to be obedient by taking three turning points:

Turning Point #1: Determine what area in life God is asking us to obey Him.
Turning Point #2: Determine what action should be taken.
Turning Point #3: Determine who we want to have in control of our lives.

Student Prayer
Ask a volunteer to pray that God will reveal the steps each person needs to take in order to be obedient.

THE EXPERIENCE

Have your D-Team members take out the local road map they have been using in the past two D-Team experiences. Ask your students: **How many different kinds of roads can you take on the map?** (Highways, county roads, city streets, dead ends, etc.) **Are any of them better than others? Why?** (The highways are better than the smaller roads because most of the time they will take us more directly to where we are going. The smaller roads take us only a little way and then we have to turn on to another small road that only takes us so far, and so on.)

There are two ways people often try to give directions. The first is to give the direction that will get your to your destination in the fastest possible. The directions are filled with short cuts and small streets, but are not always the easiest because your chances of getting lost are pretty high. The second kind of direction is the sure, fool-proof way. This way takes all the main roads and highways. These directions may take a little longer, but your chances of not getting lost are almost completely guaranteed.

Jesus tells us about a man who asked for directions and then had to decide if he would follow the fool-proof, guaranteed way of receiving eternal life or find his own way.

Prep Notes

Have your students **read Luke 18:18–27** and then discuss the following questions: **What destination did the rich young ruler want to reach?** (Eternal life) **What directions did Jesus give him?** (Obey the commandments, sell everything he owned, give it to the poor, then come follow Jesus.) **As Christians, what ultimate destination on this earth are we all looking for?** (To be more like Christ.) **What kind of directions—fastest or fool-proof—has God given us to get us there?** (God has given us the second kind of directions. The first kind of directions usually get us in trouble.)

Tell your students that even though we have these directions, there are a number of reasons why we try to find an easier route or just a route of our own. All these reasons stem from the fact that we have a sinful nature. We need to daily check to make sure that we are on the right road.

Turning Point #1: Determine what area in life God is asking us to obey Him.
If your students took the challenge from last week and figured out what area of their life God is asking them to be obedient in, they will be taking it a step further today. God has a destination for their lives and the directions involve being obedient to His commands. Today, we will determine what those commands are.

(There will probably be a mix of students in your D-Team: those who have taken the challenge from last week, those who have not taken the time to figure it out, and those who have no idea what you are talking about. Take time to ask your students these next few questions in order to bring everyone up to speed.)

1. Is there any person or situation that is taking you in a direction away from God? If yes, then who or what? (a friend, a teacher, a parent, etc.) *If no, then move on to the next question.*

2. Are you heading down God's path—the straight, open road? If yes, where is God taking you? If no, then what is stopping you?

3. Are you just getting sidetracked by something? If yes, then what is it? (busyness, school, sports, girlfriend/boyfriend, etc.) *If no, then move on to the next question.*

4. Are you avoiding God's directions because they don't take you where you want to go? If yes, then what are the two different directions? What seems to be the difference? How can they turn into the same direction? If no, then move on to the next question.

5. Is there another area in which you know God is asking you to be obedient that has not been mentioned yet? If yes, what is it? If no, then take time today to see if God shows you an area in which He wants you to be obedient.

Note that all the situations your students have mentioned are valid in God's eyes. None are ridiculous and none should be ignored. God can and will instruct students on the direction they should go with their situations if they are willing to seek His guidance.

Turning Point #2: Determine what action should be taken.
Share that, like the rich young ruler, we are asking Jesus how He will instruct us. Jesus may not speak to us in an audible voice, but He has given us a different way to know His plan. Based on the tools we studied last week—God's Word, prayer, other Christians, and our circumstances—we can determine the roads we need to take.

Ask: ***Based on what area you determined God is asking you to be obedient in, which "roads" are those tools telling you to follow?***

Discuss some of the different options we can choose from in order to be obedient to God. Ask: ***Is there someone you need to: confront? confess something to? forgive? talk to? Is there something you need to: change? give up? confess before God and man? give God control of? Is there a habit you need to get rid of?***

Allow your students some quiet time to determine at least one "road" they need to go down. Encourage them to be sure that the road of obedience they decide to take is the same road to which *all* the "tools" point, not just one of them.

Turning Point #3: Determine who we want to have in control of our lives.
Emphasize that, no matter what we are struggling with, it all comes down to this third turning point. The first two turning points are things we determined at an intellectual level. Now we must take the third turning point with our hearts. If we go through the first two turning points but don't follow through with the third, obedience, then the first two become useless head knowledge. We have to decide if we want to let God be in control of our lives.

Whenever we decide to go God's direction, we are, in essence, giving God the keys to the car. We are saying, "I know You have the best plan in mind for me. Take me the best possible way. Here is the key; I trust You with the directions."

Give each student a blank key for their key rings to remind them to let God be in control. Then ask them to pray the following prayer for themselves:

> ***I know You have the best plan in mind for me.***
> ***Take me the best possible way.***
> ***Here is the key; I trust You with the directions.***

REFLECTIONS

(5 min.)

Summarize for your students that today they learned about three turning points they can take to help them be obedient to God: they determined in which area they need to obey God, what action they should take, and who is in control.

Give your students a few moments to record honest responses to the following questions, found in their Student Notes: ***What was most meaningful to you about our experience today? What does God want you to do in response?***

Ask a student to read aloud the Summary Statements in the Student Notes.

Summary Statements

We learned today that . . .
- God wants us to be obedient in every area of our lives.
- God gives us steps of obedience to follow in order for us to grow.
- We need to choose to let God be in control of our lives on a daily basis.

Prep Notes

(10 min.)

MAKE AN IMPACT

. . . In Your Life

Have your students write down what they need to do this next week in order to be obedient. Suggest that they take time during the next week to follow through on what God is asking them to do and to be accountable to someone who will encourage them to take action. Encourage your students to put the blank key on a key ring to remind them of who is in the driver's seat if they daily give God the key to their lives.

. . . With Accountability

Have the D-Team members form pairs to become accountability partners for the week and to work on the memory verse. Have each student write out the **Unit Memory Verse**, recite it to his or her partner, and share a way the verse is meaningful in his or her life.

Prayer

Bring the students back together and close with prayer.

3. Turning Points

Review
How does God talk to us? If God wants us to obey Him, how do we know what that means for us?

Be prepared to share the area of your life in which God is asking you to obey Him.

Focus
This week you will discover how to be obedient by taking three turning points.

THE EXPERIENCE

Take out the local road map you have been using in the past two weeks. How many different kinds of roads can you take on the map? Are any of them better than others? Why?

Read Luke 18:18–27. What destination did the rich young ruler want to reach?

What directions did Jesus give him?

As Christians, what ultimate destination on this earth are we all looking for?

Summary Statements

We learned today that . . .
- God wants us to be obedient in every area of our lives.
- God gives us steps of obedience to follow in order for us to grow.
- We need to choose to let God be in control of our lives on a daily basis.

MAKE AN IMPACT

. . . In Your Life
Write down what you need to do this next week in order to be obedient. Then take time during the next week to follow through on what God is asking you to do and to be accountable to someone who will encourage you to take action. Put the blank key on a key ring to remind you of who is in the driver's seat if you daily give God the key to your life.

. . . With Accountability
With your accountability partner, talk about your responses to the "Reflection" questions. Exchange phone numbers. Call each other this week to hold each other accountable to making an impact in your life.

name _____ phone _____

Review your memory verse by writing it out in the space below. After reciting it to your partner, share a way the verse is meaningful in your life.

MEMORY VERSE
John 14:15

What kind of directions—fastest or fool-proof—has God given us to get us there?

Turning Point #1: Determine what area in life God is asking us to obey Him.

Take some time to determine (or confirm) the area God is asking you to be obedient in by answering these questions:

1. Is there any person or situation that is taking you in a direction away from God? If yes, then who or what is it? If no, then move on to the next question.

2. Are you heading down God's path—the straight, open road? If yes, where is God taking you? If no, then what is stopping you?

3. Are you just getting sidetracked by something? If yes, then what is it? If no, then move on to the next question.

4. Are you avoiding God's directions because they don't take you where you want to go? If yes, then what are the two different directions? What seems to be the difference? How can they turn into the same direction? If no, then move on to the next question.

5. Is there another area in which you know God is asking you to be obedient that has not been mentioned yet? If yes, what is it? If no, then take time today to see if God shows you an area in which He wants you to be obedient.

Turning Point #2: Determine what action should be taken.

Based on what you determined God is asking you to be obedient in, which "roads" are those tools telling you to follow?

Is there someone you need to: confront? confess something to? forgive? talk to?

Is there something you need to: change? give up? confess before God and man? give God control of?

Is there a habit you need to get rid of?

Turning Point #3: Determine who we want to have in control of our lives.

Your blank key will remind you to let God be in control. Pray the following prayer for yourself if you decide to let God be in control of your life:

Dear God,
I know that You have the best plan in mind for me;
take me the best possible way.
Here is the key; I trust You with the directions.

REFLECTIONS

Today you learned about three turning points you can take to help you be obedient to God. You determined in which area you need to obey God, what action you should take, and who is in control.

What was most meaningful to you about our experience today?

What does God want you to do in response?

Shepherding Summary Form

Complete this form immediately after every meeting and give a copy to your ministry director or small groups coordinator.

ATTENDANCE

Leader:

Apprentice leader:

Members present: Guests filling the "empty chair":

Members absent:

Starting core number:

ACTIVITY SUMMARY
Briefly describe how you incorporated the CLEAR values listed below.

Christ—How was Christ made the central focus of your time together?

Listen— Were you able to meet the students' needs to be heard? What concerns arose?

Empty chair—Are students praying for specific friends they could invite to join the small group? How are you fostering an openness to new members?

Affirm—In what ways were you able to affirm your students?

Read and pray—How effective was your time in the Word and in prayer together?

CELEBRATION
What's happening in your small group that you'd like to celebrate or note? What problems or questions do you need help with?

WILLOW CREEK
RESOURCES

This resource was created to serve you.

It is just one of many ministry tools that are part of the Willow Creek Resources® line, published by the Willow Creek Association together with Zondervan Publishing House. The Willow Creek Association was created in 1992 to serve a rapidly growing number of churches from all across the denominational spectrum that are committed to helping unchurched people become fully devoted followers of Christ. There are now more than 2,500 WCA member churches worldwide.

The Willow Creek Association links like-minded leaders with each other and with strategic vision, information, and resources in order to build prevailing churches. Here are some of the ways it does that:

• **Church Leadership Conferences**—3 1/2 -day events, held at Willow Creek Community Church in South Barrington, IL, that are being used by God to help church leaders find new and innovative ways to build prevailing churches that reach unchurched people.

• **The Leadership Summit**—a once-a-year event designed to increase the leadership effectiveness of pastors, ministry staff, volunteer church leaders, and Christians in business.

• **Willow Creek Resources®**—to provide churches with a trusted channel of ministry resources in areas of leadership, evangelism, spiritual gifts, small groups, drama, contemporary music, and more. For more information, call Willow Creek Resources® at 800/876-7335. Outside the US call 610/532-1249.

• *WCA News*—a bimonthly newsletter to inform you of the latest trends, resources, and information on WCA events from around the world.

• *The Exchange*—our classified ads publication to assist churches in recruiting key staff for ministry positions.

• **The Church Associates Directory**—to keep you in touch with other WCA member churches around the world.

• *WillowNet*—an Internet service that provides access to hundreds of Willow Creek messages, drama scripts, songs, videos and multimedia suggestions. The system allows users to sort through these elements and download them for a fee.

• *Defining Moments*—a monthly audio journal for church leaders, in which Lee Strobel asks Bill Hybels and other Christian leaders probing questions to help you discover biblical principles and transferable strategies to help maximize your church's potential.

For conference and membership information please write or call:

Willow Creek Association
P.O. Box 3188
Barrington, IL 60011-3188
ph: (847) 765-0070
fax: (847) 765-5046
www.willowcreek.org

0597